CORNISH

FOLK
TALES

CORNISH
FOLK
TALES

MIKE O'CONNOR

First published 2010

The History Press
The Mill, Brimscombe Port
Stroud, Gloucestershire, GL5 2QG
www.thehistorypress.co.uk

Reprinted 2011, 2013

© Mike O'Connor, 2011

The right of Mike O'Connor to be identified as the Author
of this work has been asserted in accordance with the
Copyrights, Designs and Patents Act 1988.

British Library Cataloguing in Publication Data.
A catalogue record for this book is available from the British Library.

ISBN 978 0 7524 5066 7

Typesetting and origination by The History Press
Printed and bound by TJ International Ltd, Padstow, Cornwall

CONTENTS

ACKNOWLEDGEMENTS

A storyteller is a link in a chain, a reed in a river, a cloud in a storm of words. Tales are heard, learned, adapted and passed on. I acknowledge my place as a bearer of this tradition. I offer thanks and blessings to:

Cornish storytellers of old, especially Anthony James, Billy Foss and William Hicks.

Their chroniclers, especially William Bottrell, Robert Hunt and Enys Tregarthen.

Storytelling mentors and friends: Tina O'Connor, Barbara Griggs, Del and Pippa Reid, Mike Rust, Taffy Thomas MBE, Kathy Wallis and the late Duncan Williamson.

Cornish language advisers: Jenefer Lowe, Elizabeth Stewart and Pol Hodge of MAGA Kernow, the Cornish Language Partnership.

ILLUSTRATIONS

The lovely cover illustration is by Katherine Soutar-Caddick, and it depicts the flight of Trevillian from the innundation of Lyonesse. 'Excalibur' is by Barbara Griggs (© 2009). Framed illustrations were by Cooper for the 'Legend Land' books of 1922. The small illustrations of piskeys, giants and the like were drawn by Joseph Blight for William Bottrell's books of folk tales of 1873 and 1880. The drawing of the Giant Bolster was drawn by the well-known illustrator and caricaturist George Cruikshank (1792-1878) for Robert Hunt's collection of 1865. These illustrations inevitably have a long and much-loved association with Cornish folk tales. Other line drawings are from Arthur G. Langdon's *Old Cornish Crosses* of 1896; John Blight's *Ancient Crosses and other Antiquities* of 1858; John Ayrton Paris' *A Guide to the Mount's Bay and the Land's End* of 1824; and Tregellas' *Peeps into the Haunts and Homes of the Rural Population of Cornwall* of 1879. Other woodcuts are from the Dover Pictorial Archive and are reproduced in accordance with their terms and conditions.

FOREWORD

This book brings together tales from many Cornish sources, the majority of which are documentary. Importantly, some are from Anthony James of Cury. Anthony and his son travelled Cornwall in the late eighteenth and early nineteenth centuries, telling tales, singing songs and playing tunes. This book is their travelogue.

Anthony James was probably born around 1767 in or near Cury, a hamlet on the Lizard. He was possibly orphaned when still a minor. He learned the fiddle when young, and could play at dances and sing to entertain. He joined the 32nd (Cornwall) Regiment of Foot, perhaps by 1794. The regiment was a precursor of the Duke of Cornwall's Light Infantry and at this time was quartered in Plymouth. In 1795 the regiment served in Cork, but in 1796 sailed to the West Indies. On ship Anthony would have learned nautical tales and heard the ship's fiddler playing dance tunes. In 1796 and 1797 the regiment served in Haiti and the Bahamas. However, it seems that Anthony was blinded and repatriated. A military pensioner, Anthony was entitled to accommodation in Stoke Military Hospital, Stonehouse, Devonport (built in 1791). He used Stoke as winter quarters, but in summer he crossed the Tamar, a fiddle under his arm. In Cornwall he was a travelling 'droll teller', guided by his son and living on his tales, songs and tunes. He was undoubtedly helped by the Cornish love of storytelling, including 'epic tales'.[1]

In about 1865 William Bottrell wrote to Robert Hunt:

> He neither begged nor offered anything for sale, but was sure of a
> welcome to bed and board in every house he called at. He would

seldom stop in the same house more than one night, not because he had exhausted his stories, or 'eaten his welcome,' but because it required all his time to visit his acquaintances once in the year. The old man was called 'Uncle' Anthony James. (Uncle is a term of respect.)

Anthony James used to arrive every year in St Levan parish about the end of August. Soon after he reached my father's house, he would stretch himself on the 'chimney-stool,' and sleep until supper-time. When the old man had finished his frugal meal of bread and milk, he would tune his fiddle and ask if 'missus' would like to hear him sing her favourite ballad. As soon as my dear mother told him how pleased she would be, Uncle Anthony would go through the 'woeful hunting'; (Chevy Chase), from beginning to end, accompanied by the boy and the fiddle. I expect the air was his own composition, as every verse was a different tune.

James' repertoire included 'The Streams of Lovely Nancy', 'Cold Blows the Wind', 'Ann Tremellan' (c.f. 'Barbara Allen') and 'Babes in the Wood'. Bottrell continued:

> Yet the grand resource was the stories in which the supernatural bore great part. The story of Luty [sic] finding the mermaid, who gave his descendants the power to break the spell of witchcraft, was one of this old man's tales, which he seemed to believe; and he regarded the conjurer with as much respect as the bard might the priest in olden time.

Hunt then wrote, 'in 1829 there still existed two of those droll tellers.'[2] Also in about 1869, Bottrell described Anthony as a travelling droll teller who played the 'crowd' and sang traditional songs 'some forty years ago.'[3] James told the tales of 'Lutey and the Mermaid' and 'Drakes Droll' and sang 'old ballads all about Sir Francis and privateering... In his youth he had been a soldier and had visited many foreign lands... who takes a turn round the country every Summer and passes the Winters in Plymouth, with other old pensioners.'

Revd John Skinner wrote of a blind fiddler and 'a young scraper', his son, usual musicians at Assemblies in Bodmin but not present in November 1797.[4] That they were then absent matches the notes that James wintered in Plymouth.

Between 1816 and 1846 William Sandys heard 'Richard of Taunton Dean' from an old blind fiddler 'who used to accompany it on his instrument in an original and humorous manner; a representative of the old minstrels!'[5] This was probably at Carwythenack, just four miles from Cury.[6] Sandys collected many traditional carols and James could have been one of his sources.

Most of the 'supporting cast' are also real and are accurately, if briefly, represented. These include William Allen, Henry Boase, Caleb Boney, William Bottrell, John Davey, Joseph Emidy, Billy Foss, Parson Hawker, William Hicks, John Old, Richard Parkyn, James Polkinghorne, Henry Quick, William Sandys, John Skinner and Tommy Trudgeon. References to Cornish customs and folklore are factual. The only liberty taken is to place events in the same year so as to give a coherent narrative and draw certain characters into James' ambit.

I have written the tales as I tell them. I have not imposed the language of antiquarian or other sources, nor have I attempted to reproduce an artificial Cornish dialect. That fine vernacular has continued to evolve since the tales were first noted, and also has regional variation within Cornwall.

A late form of the Cornish language was still used in some contexts by farmers and fishermen in the far west at the time of this travelogue. However, it was then in serious decline and was largely oral. There is no easy way to depict the complexities of the language. Its usages and spelling had been evolving for centuries, giving the variations inevitably found in quotations and place names. Thus to give a consistent, if necessarily stylized, representation of the Cornish language of 1800, I have left quotations in the late Cornish forms in which they were noted and used place names as then known. I have rendered speech and chapter numerals in late period Standard Written Form Cornish.

As described above, Anthony was a droll teller. In Cornish dialect a 'droll' is an oral story – it can be delivered in prose, in rhymes, in song or in any combination of these. Anthony and his son played the 'crowd' and were 'crowders'. These words are Cornish dialect for fiddle and fiddler. But 'crowd' is also short for 'crowdy-crawn', a sieve-rim drum, known in the West Country since the thirteenth century. The context usually makes the meaning clear.

In the early nineteenth century the Industrial Revolution brought huge changes to parts of Cornwall. In many places the once-rural landscape was dominated by mining and a common feeling was that the 'old ways' were dying. As the gloomy Zennor poet Henry Quick wrote:

> Our Cornish drolls are dead, each one;
> The fairies from their haunts have gone:
> There's scarce a witch in all the land,
> The world has grown so learn'd and grand.

Anthony James seems to have been fondly remembered as a representative of a bygone culture. But his stories and songs have survived. Despite Quick's pessimism, the drolls are not dead.

So let us start our journey. Once again we can travel the lanes of Cornwall with Anthony James. Cornwall is a special land with a unique culture. Once independent, it has its own classical literature, its own music and its own Celtic language. In many places we would begin 'once upon a time'. But this is Cornwall, so 'Y'n termyn eus passyes…'

Notes

1 Baring Gould, S., *The Vicar of Morwenstow: A Life of Robert Stephen Hawker, M.A.* (Henry S. King, London, 1876) pp. 54, 55 refer.

2 Hunt, R., *Popular Romances of the West of England* (J.C. Hotten, London, 1865) Vol. 1 pp. 26, 27 refer.

3 Bottrell, W., *Traditions and Hearthside Stories of West Cornwall* (Penzance, 1870, 1873 & 1880) Series 1 pp. 60, 61 and Series 3 p. 72 refer.

4 Skinner, Revd John, *A West Country Tour, Being the Diary of a Tour Through the Counties of Somerset, Devon and Cornwall in 1797* (date unknown) [Skinner (1772-1839), rector of Camerton in Somerset was an antiquarian and archaeologist. On 15 November 1797 he reached Falmouth (See p. 78 of 96).]

5 Dixon, J.H., *Ancient Poems, Ballads, and Songs of the Peasantry of England* (Percy Society, London, 1846)

6 Sandys (1792-1874) married Harriette Hill of Carwythenack, Constantine, in 1816.

THE JOURNEY

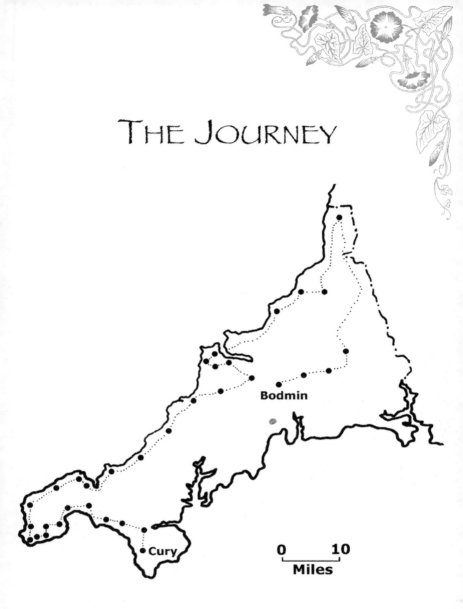

Bodmin

Cury

0   10
Miles

1

Onan

CURY

It was a spring morning full of promise and birdsong. The day was sky-bright and clear. A child standing in the lane looked up in surprise as a figure came into sight. The hamlet of Cury saw few visitors. To the north and south were byways to the farms at Nanfan and Sowanna. Away to the west was the sea, always audible. But from the east came the stranger.

The sun was at his back as he walked down from White Cross. His clothes were weather-beaten; once they had been military uniform. Over his shoulder was a canvas sack. At his left side a green cloth bag hung from his belt. His right hand held a stick that constantly swept to right and left, sensing the grass verge by the dry-stone wall. Then he stopped and ran his fingers across the stones.

'What are you doing?' asked the child.

'That'll be the town hedge', said the stranger, smiling. Dry-stone walls are always called hedges in Cornwall.

The boy saw how the irregular field-stones in the wall had given way to a neater, vertical pattern.

'What's your name, boy?'

'Anthony James Vingoe,' he chanted, 'but Mam calls me Jamie. What's yours?'

The man paused, then smiled broadly.

'My name's almost the same', he said. 'It's just Anthony James. Where do you live, Jamie?'

'Up Churchtown', said the boy.

'Please Jamie, would you take me to meet your mam?' said Anthony.

'Wait,' he continued, 'let me put my hand on your shoulder.'

'What for?' said Jamie.

'I can't see, so you must be my eyes. Be sure that you tell me when we reach your house, and don't call out.'

Half a mile later they stopped at a small cottage. The irregular thatched roof was in need of maintenance, but a wisp of smoke curled upwards from the chimney. The stranger opened the bag at his belt and from it took a violin. He put it to his chin and drew the bow across the strings. The music was swift and light, but soulful all the same. The notes echoed through the open door.

From inside there was a cry that was a laugh and a shout all together, and a young woman ran to the door, a babe in her arms.

'Anthony James,' she cried, 'they said you were dead!'

Then she stopped, inches from him. 'Oh my love!' she said, 'What have they done to your eyes?'

Their embrace was long, full of smiles and tears.

'Would you have some nettle tea?' said the young mother.

'Martha,' said Anthony, 'there are two things a man should never refuse from a good woman, and the first of them is a cup of tea.'

'You old rogue,' she said, 'what's the second?'

'Another cup of tea, of course,' he replied, 'what did you expect? Jamie, guide me to the table. Then, Martha, I'll tell you my story if you tell me yours. May I sit down?'

'You need to rest before midday?' she asked.

'I just walked from Plymouth!' was the reply.

At the table Martha nervously took Anthony by the hand.

'I've married,' she said, 'Alan Vingoe, from the farm. They told me you were dead. I knew I was expecting. What could I do?'

'You did the right thing,' said Anthony, 'even if it hurts me to say it. I couldn't keep you now. I'm no match for any maid.'

Martha looked questioningly. 'They said you'd run off to sea, couldn't face your responsibilities.'

'Your father and mother?' asked Anthony.

'Both long gone', she sighed.

Anthony drew a deep breath. 'You shouldn't speak ill of the dead, but I can't help but think your father and the recruiting sergeant had words. Your old man was never too keen on me. The soldiers were up Cross Lanes, the Wheel Inn, and they seemed to have money to burn, enough to buy me ale. When I woke there were shackles on my ankles and I was on my way to Devonport. Since then I've been half way round the world with the 32nd Regiment of Foot. They kept us overseas so we wouldn't run away; Cork, Haiti and the Bahamas. I only got home 'cause Johnny Frenchman put chain shot in the rigging of our transport and a spar fell on my head.'

'And now?'

'Now I'm a pensioner of the quartermaster general. If I were in London they'd call me a Chelsea Pensioner. They put me in the Royal Military Hospital in Stonehouse. Now I'm fit enough to get about; so come the spring they let me go on the road. In the winter I'll go back to Devonport and reclaim my bed.'

'But how will you live?'

'I could just sit at Stonehouse with my memories. But a man will choke soon enough on army grub and old dreams. This is my land; I'd rather be here. I've enough tales and tunes for all of Cornwall.'

Martha smiled, 'A travelling droll teller! Just like old Billy Foss from Sancreed.'

'That's right,' said Anthony, 'and a good man is "Frosty" Foss. He used to go to the feasts all round Penwith, and was well entertained in the public houses for the sake of his drolls. But now he tells more tales at his forge, or in his mason's yard out the back. Anyway, Cornwall is big enough for both of us.'

'What's a droll?' asked Jamie.

'It's just what they call the old stories', said Anthony. 'Sometimes they're spoken; sometimes they take the form of songs; sometimes both.'

So all afternoon, by the fireside, Anthony played his fiddle, sang songs and told tales. As if by magic, around him gathered more children. Soon to them, as to all the world, he was their 'Uncle Anthony'. Some tales were funny, some were magic, many were of Cornwall and some were of far-away places. But somehow, what-ever happened and wherever Anthony led his listeners, at the end of each tale they found themselves safely home again. As Anthony sowed his seeds in words and music, Jamie was captivated by the images that grew in his mind.

At the end of the day the room darkened as a figure filled the door.

'Alan!' exclaimed Martha.

'Well, I'll be blowed! Anthony James, back from the dead.'

Alan looked at Martha, then at Anthony.

'Well, Anthony James,' he said, 'you're not stopping here.'

Anthony gave a wry smile. 'Nor did I think to', he said.

Martha spoke urgently. 'Alan, he could sleep in the shed, couldn't he? Just tonight.'

'Yes, just tonight', said Alan. 'But the door'll be bolted, mind.'

'I want no trouble, I'll be gone before dawn', said Anthony.

That evening was clear and still, and the stars were very bright. The sound of the sea filled the heavens. With the dawn it was Martha who found that the door of the cottage was unbolted. It was neighbours who heard her crying out, 'Jamie, Jamie! Where are you Jamie?'

2

Dew

CARWYTHENACK

A worried crowd had gathered outside the cottage at Churchtown. Occasionally one or other figure would peer into the distance; the conversation ebbed and flowed. Suddenly their attention was drawn by a shout from the direction of White Cross.

Jamie Vingoe, suspended by his belt, was wriggling like an eel. Anthony James struggled to keep his balance, holding the boy in his left hand, and feeling the way with the stick held in his right hand. From a distance of a hundred yards the crowd could hear the boy crying out, between sobs and intakes of breath, 'I… don't… want… to… go… home.'

They arrived outside the cottage. There Martha gratefully seized the errant boy. Despite being home Jamie still seemed comfortable in his mother's embrace.

'Jamie,' said Anthony James, 'if you ever, ever, want to come on the road with me in the future, you must come home now. You cannot just run away from everything you've ever known. Life won't let you, I know that, and anyway you owe it to your folks to ask them first.'

'But I want to go with you' sobbed the lad.

'Don't you love your Mum and Dad?' asked Anthony.

'Yes.'

'Don't you like it at home?'

'Yes.'

'But you want to come with me?'

'Yes, I could help…'

There was an uneasy silence, punctuated with snuffles from Jamie.

Alan Vingoe spoke next. 'He's too young to work on the land. He's too daft to work in the house. He might just learn something.'

'No!' cried Martha.

'Please mum…' cried Jamie.

'No', repeated his mother.

As the debate continued, Anthony James quietly took a pace backwards, turned and headed back up the lane towards the rising sun. No one seemed to notice his going.

He was sitting in the hedge deep in the shade of the elder tree at White Cross when a small figure came scurrying up the lane. The lad carried a bag on his shoulder, but ran with great urgency. By the time Anthony James extricated himself from the hedge, the figure had passed him and was heading up towards Cury Cross Lanes.

'Hey Jamie,' said Anthony, 'wait for me.'

'They said I could come', said Jamie. 'Oh! Why are you crying?' They tramped through the rest of the morning. As they walked they worked out the ways of guiding a blind man across Cornwall. Much depended on the going underfoot. Towns sometimes had cobbled streets or flags. Where roads were regularly used by carts, either for tin ore or for farm produce, the surface was often crushed stone. Lanes were often just rough earth, sometimes pitted and puddled. Many tracks were just used by pack horses or donkeys and they were often winding and uneven. Where the going was good Anthony could walk unaided, his stick identifying the kerb, hedge or wall. Sometimes they would walk independently, each holding the opposite end of a piece of hairy string left over after binding the stooks of corn at harvest time. Where the going was more difficult they would hold hands, or Anthony would place a hand on Jamie's shoulder. Sometimes Jamie would hold one end of Anthony's walking stick to guide him. But such was their joy at being together, the going did not seem to matter.

As they walked they swapped jokes, riddles and tall tales; the very best way to make the miles fly past. Once again Jamie noticed that without thinking he visualized the stories as Anthony told them. 'It's not like in books,' said Anthony, 'a storyteller says just enough for the listener to create the images in their own mind. If you say too much you can spoil it.'

By midday they had reached the Helford River. They sat under the trees, ate bread and cheese, and Jamie watched the sparkling water.

WILLIAM SANDYS

That afternoon they reached the farm of Carwythenack. 'Lead me to the door,' said Anthony James. He knocked on the door and in a while it opened. Anthony heard a female voice call out, 'It's just two beggars, shall I send them on their way?' But by then he had taken his fiddle from its bag and had started to play. Jamie heard a man's voice answer in a London accent, 'No, Harriette, ask them inside.'

They were shown into the farm kitchen. A pretty young woman stood nervously in the corner. An alert young man spoke to them. 'Come in. You, lad, show your dad the way. Sit at the table.'

Jamie started, 'He's…'

'Shhh!' said Anthony, 'Thank you sir. What is your will? A tale or a tune, a song or a story?'

The man replied, 'I hope I shall hear all of those in a moment. But come, sir, we have not yet been introduced.'

Anthony smiled, 'Sir, I am Anthony James of Cury, and late of the 32nd Regiment of Foot, and this is young Jamie, who is my guide and my best friend.'

'Splendid,' came the reply, 'my name is William Sandys and this is Miss Harriette, my fiancée, and the heiress of Carwythenack.'

'My congratulations to you both,' said Anthony, 'I'm sure you make a handsome couple. I am happy your courtship pleases you both. But let me tell you of one that did not.'

Anthony held his fiddle in the crook of his arm and started to play in jig time. After a few bars he started to sing as he played. 'Excellent,' exclaimed William Sandys as Anthony sang of a farmer's unsuccessful but amusing courtship of a parson's daughter. Every so often the chorus came round, and everyone joined in: 'Dumble-dum deary, dumble-dum deary, dumble-dum, dumble-dum, dumble-dum dee!'

At the end of the song the poor farmer retreated in confusion, but in the farmhouse of Carwythenack all were laughing fit to bust at the tale of Richard of Taunton Dean. Small ale was brought in, and more food. The evening passed in good humoured self-entertainment. Although William Sandys had a London accent, he knew a lot about Cornwall and could tell a fine tale himself. 'Just like the old minstrels.' Sandys laughed, 'Do you know any more?'

'Well,' said Anthony, 'many Cornish ports have stories of mermaids. I learned this tale from fishermen on the Lizard...'

LUTEY AND THE MERMAID

Once there was an old fisherman named Lutey. He divided his time between farming and fishing, as the weather and season took him. Well, one summer evening Lutey had finished his work early, so he took his dog Venture for a walk on the sands to see if he could find any flotsam or jetsam. But as he walked on the sand he heard a sad, sad cry. It sounded like a woman or child in distress.

On the sands were rocks. They were covered at high tide, but at low tide they were far from the sea, with rock pools between them. The cry seemed to come from the rocks so Lutey went there to see if he could help. At first he could see no one, but on the seaward side, in a rock pool, he saw something that nearly left him speechless.

Lying on a ledge in a rock pool was the most beautiful woman he had ever seen. Her hair was long and golden. Her eyes were green and they sparkled like sun on the waves. This beautiful girl was gazing sadly at the sea and occasionally gave the pitiful cry that had first attracted Lutey. She was clearly in great distress.

At first, Lutey tried to be subtle, but could not attract her attention. Eventually he called out, 'What's the matter, miss? What are you doing here by yourself?' He spoke softly, but the girl cried with terror and disappeared into the rock pool.

Lutey thought she had drowned. But when he looked into the pool, he saw her hair, then her head, shoulders, body, and then a fish's tail! He trembled with fear for he realised he had found a mermaid! The mermaid raised her head above the water, and gazed at him with her bright green eyes.

However, she was just as frightened as he was so he spoke again, for it's always best to be kind to mermaids and not offend them. If they are angry there is no knowing what they may do.

'Please don't be frightened,' said Lutey, 'I only want to help.' So the mermaid floated higher and higher, and eventually was brave enough to climb up and perch on a rock. Her long hair fell about her, and in one hand she held a comb and in the other mirror.

'Just a few hours ago,' she said, 'I was with my husband and children, as happy as a mermaid could be. Then we all went to rest in

a cave at Kynance Cove. My husband went to sleep. The children went to play in the waves and I was left alone. But after a while the sweet scent of flowers came to me from the gardens of your world, and I felt I must go and see them.'

'I swam here, but I found I could not get near the flowers; but I thought I would rest here and comb my hair, and breathe in their sweetness.'

'I was dreaming of your world, then I suddenly found the tide was far out. I was so frightened. If my husband wakes and misses me he will be angry, for mermen are very jealous. He will be hungry, too, and if he finds no supper ready he will eat some of the children!'

'No,' cried Lutey, *'surely he wouldn't do such a thing!'*

'Mermen are gluttons', she said. *'They gobble up their children in a moment if their meals are late. I have only ten little ones left, and they will all be gone if I don't get home before he wakes!'*

'Don't worry my dear. The tide will be soon in.'

'I can't wait', she cried, tears running down her cheeks. *'Please help me! Carry me to the sea; help me for ten minutes, and I will make you rich for life. Ask of me anything you want, and it shall be yours.'*

Lutey was so enthralled by the beauty of the mermaid that he would have done anything she asked him. He stooped to pick her up.

'Take this,' she said, giving him her pearl comb, *'take this, to prove to you that you have not been dreaming, and that I will do for you what I have said. Whenever you want me, comb the sea three times with this, and call me by my name, "Morvena", and I will come to you. Now take me to the sea.'*

Stooping again, he picked her up in his arms. She clung tightly to him, twining her long arms around his neck. *'Tell me your wishes,'* she said sweetly, *'would you like long life, strength and riches?'*

'No thank you, lady' said Lutey thoughtfully. *'But I'd dearly love to be able to remove the spells of the witches, to have power over spirits to make them tell me all I want to know so I can help others, and I'd like these gifts to carry on in my family forever.'*

'Your wishes are granted,' cried the mermaid, *'and as you have been so selfless, I promise that your family will always be provided for.'*

☙

Lutey trudged on, while the mermaid held him ever closer and told him all about the delights of the world under the sea. Soon they passed the water's edge and Lutey started to wade out into the deeper water.

'Come with me, Lutey,' she cried, 'come with me to our caves and palaces; there are riches, beauty and everything any mortal can want. Come to be one of us whose lives are all love, and sunshine, and merriment.'

The breakers they wanted to reach were not far off. Lutey was tempted to go with the mermaid; her green eyes had utterly bewitched him. She saw that he was almost in her power. She clasped her long fingers round his neck and pressed her cool lips to his.

Another instant and Lutey would have gone, but at that moment there came from the shore the sound of a dog barking. It was Venture, Lutey's dog, left behind on the sand. Lutey turned to look. Venture was at the water's edge. Beyond, on the cliff, stood his home, the windows reflecting against the sun, his garden, and the country looking green and beautiful; the smoke was rising from his chimney. All of a sudden the mermaid's spell was broken. He remembered all the old tales he had heard of the power of mermaids and their ability to seduce humans.

'Let me go!' cried Lutey, trying to lower the mermaid into the water. But she clung on even more tightly.

'Let me go!' he yelled again, and from his belt he took his knife. As the steel flashed before the mermaid's eyes she slipped away from him, as merfolk cannot abide steel. But as she swam slowly away, she sang, and the words came floating back to Lutey, 'Farewell, farewell. I give you nine years. Then, my love, I'll come back for you!'

Lutey waded back to the land, but he was so shaken by everything that had happened it was almost too much for him. When he reached the shore he just managed to scramble up the beach to a cave where he kept some treasures he had smuggled from time to time, including some brandy that he'd hidden from the excise man. To fortify himself he took a long drink and then he fell into a deep sleep.

Of course, his good woman, poor old Ann Betty Lutey, was in a dreadful state when supper time was past and her husband had not returned. All night she watched for him. When breakfast time came and still there was no sign of him, she set off to look for him.

Ann Betty did not have to search far. Outside the cave she found Venture sleeping. As the dog was seldom far from his master, she looked inside and there she found her husband. He was still sound asleep. Ann Betty was vexed at having been frightened, and she shook him roughly. 'Lutey, get up at once!' she cried. 'Where've 'ee been? What 'ave 'ee been doing?'

Lutey sat up. 'Who are you?' he said. 'Are you the beautiful maiden come for me? Are you Morvena?'

'What are you talking about? You haven't called me beautiful for thirty years, and I'm not called Morvena. I'm Ann Betty Lutey, your wife, and if you don't know me, you must be out of your mind.'

'My dear Ann Betty,' said the old Lutey solemnly, 'if you're my lawful wife you've only just escaped being left a widow.'

'Come in and have breakfast,' said Ann Betty sternly, 'and if you're not better then, I'll send for the doctor. I think your brain is addled.'

Lutey went in to have his breakfast. As he ate he told his wife about his adventure the evening before, but he told her to keep it all a secret. But before long Ann Betty gossiped it all round the parish, producing the mermaid's comb as evidence.

Soon old Lutey was besieged by the sick and sorry for miles around and he found that his wishes had indeed been granted. He could heal the sick and undo evil spells, and he became well known across the land. The mermaid was true to all her promises. He got all his wishes, and neither he nor his descendants were ever poor.

But nine years later, on a calm moonlight night, Lutey, who by then had forgotten all about the mermaid, went fishing with a friend. There was not a breath of wind and the sea was like glass. Then suddenly the sea rose round the boat in a huge wave with a thick crest of foam. In the midst of the foam was Morvena, as lovely as ever, her arms outstretched, her clear green eyes fixed on Lutey.

For a moment he looked at her, then, as if under a spell, he rose in the boat and turned his face towards the open sea. 'My time is come', he said, and he stepped out of the boat. For a moment Lutey and the mermaid were seen in each other's arms, but then they sank below the surface and the sea was smooth again.

Lutey was never seen again. And since that day, although the family has prospered, no matter how careful they are, every ninth year one of Lutey's descendants is claimed by the sea.

HEROD AND THE COCK

The stars were shining through the kitchen window when Sandys asked, 'What about Christmas carols? The oldest and the best seem to be preserved in Cornwall when they have died out elsewhere.'

'Well,' said Anthony, 'I know the carols my grandmother used to sing.'

'That's good', said Sandys and Anthony James started:

When Herod in Jerusalem
Did reign in princely throne,
Strange tidings then were brought to him
Of a King lately born;
The which did much torment his mind,
So strange a thing should be,
That then amongst the Jews should reign
A greater King than he.

He told how the three wise men saw a star in the sky. They knew it meant that a great King had been born, and they went to pay homage. They followed the star until they saw a palace. They thought this be must where the King was. But there they found King Herod, just sitting down to his first ever Christmas dinner – though he didn't know it at the time. On the plate was a fine cockerel, potatoes, parsnips, carrots, Brussels sprouts and lashings of gravy.

The first wise man, who was very wise, said, 'We're looking for a King.'

The second wise man, who was fairly wise, said, 'We're looking for a great King.'

The third wise man, who may have been wise but was certainly not intelligent, said, 'We're looking for a King far greater than You!'

Herod thumped his fist on the table, full of rage. 'There is no King greater that me!' he said. 'If there is a King greater than me then this roasted cock that lies in the dish will crow three times.' Then they all looked at the cockerel. There was a pop as its head appeared from inside its neck. Soon it 'thrustened' and grew plump, and feathers grew where not long before they had been plucked out. Slowly it stretched out one leg and splashed in the gravy. Then it stretched the other and put it down between the Brussels sprouts. It staggered to its feet. One, two, three times it crowed.

So they all knew that a great King had indeed been born. Herod said, 'When you find this King be sure to tell me where he is so I can pay him homage as well.'

Now you all know that the wise men found baby Jesus with Joseph and Mary away in a manger. There they gave the baby Jesus the first ever Christmas presents. And in a dream an angel told them that Herod was full of envy and malice, so they went home a different way.

William Sandys was beside himself with excitement. 'Did you know they told that tale to congregations in Bodmin in the fifteenth century?'

'I just know my grandmother told it to me!' said Anthony James, 'Would you like another?'

THE MIRACULOUS HARVEST

Joseph and Mary heard that the evil King Herod was looking for the baby Jesus. They fled on the road to Egypt with baby Jesus on the back of a donkey. On the way they passed a field where a poor farmer was sowing seed. He was very busy, but he still found time to wave and smile at the baby.

The Holy Child smiled back and waved at the farmer in his field. Straight away the seeds started to grow. By the time that the Holy Family were out of sight, the corn had grown and ripened and the farmer was able to take his scythe to harvest the crop.

Then there was the sound of marching feet; it was Herod with his soldiers. He called to the farmer, 'Have you seen a mother and father with a baby on a donkey?'

The farmer said, 'The truth it must be told, I have seen them.'

'Good,' said Herod, 'when did you see them?'

The farmer said, 'The truth it must be told. When I saw them I was just sowing the seed for this crop that I am now harvesting.' So Herod thought it must have been a whole season before, and he went back to his palace. So it was that Herod was defeated, the Holy Family continued safely into Egypt and the salvation of us all was assured.

'What a wonderful story', said Harriette.

'Wonderful indeed,' said William Sandys, 'Anthony and Jamie, that was excellent. Let me show you to our guest room. You deserve a good night's sleep.'

3

TRei

HELSTON

Next morning Anthony James rose unaccountably early. Jamie complained as Anthony swiftly bade farewell to Mr Sandys and strode down the road towards Helston. The air was chill and dew clung to every blade of grass, gleaming in the early sun.

THE HAL AN TOW

As they reached the outskirts of Helston, Jamie saw an amazing poster pinned to a door. It read:

HELSTON FURRY DAY A Grand PROCESSION will parade the town in the following order: Outrider on Horseback, A Company of Sharp shooters from the Seat of War in full uniform. A strong Body of Police. AUNT MARY MOSES, on a White Palfrey, with her Squires and Attendants. BAND. Constables with their Staffs of Office. A REAL BLACK TURK, dressed in the full uniform of a Turkish Warrior, armed with a Turkish blunderbuss, with which he killed 15 Russians in one engagement. HIS WORSHIP THE MAYOR OF ST JOHN'S drawn by six Jerusalem Ponies, Attended by his Secretary and Groom, Coachman and two Postillions, in gorgeous liveries. CITY CRIER in a Carriage and Pair. THE

COUNCIL-MEN TWO and TWO. The Procession will enter the
Town Hall at 9 o'clock precisely.

Jamie had just read to the bottom and was thinking that it looked
very grand, if unlikely, when he was startled to hear raucous singing and shouting. A motley band of youths ran towards them.
They wore a startling variety of ragged costumes. One had his face
covered in soot; another wore a voluminous dress. Drums were
banged and the words 'a forfeit, a forfeit' were repeated worryingly
often. Jamie clung to Anthony's legs, but Anthony just smiled,
took out his fiddle and started to play. To a man the revellers
started to sing; the chorus was especially loud.

'Hal an Tow, jolly rumbelow,' it echoed. Then as quickly as they
had appeared, the singers ran off down the hill.

'Who are they?' asked Jamie.

'That was him, the mock mayor of St John's and his court', said
Anthony. 'It's called the Hal an Tow. First thing on 8 May they go
round settling old scores. If you've crossed them in the last twelve-
month, well at best they wake you up early.'

'And at worst?' asked Jamie.

'They, ahem, invite you to jump across the river down below the
town.'

'And?' said Jamie.

'The water there is about twenty foot wide!' Anthony continued, 'But it's all fun really.'

The Furry Dance

They hurried on to the Angel Hotel, where another crowd had
gathered despite the early hour. Anthony again put his fiddle to his
chin. The crowd swiftly separated into couples in a line. Guided
by Jamie, Anthony James set off down the street, and the crowd
followed, dancing every step. For eight bars they danced forwards
together, then for another eight they joyfully spun and twisted
in each other's arms. Soon the chain wove its way into lanes and

alleys, then even through houses, as it danced from one street to the next. Nor did it stop. For the best part of five miles, Anthony James played his fiddle until he found himself back at the Angel. Jamie was tired, but the dancers seemed inexhaustible. At the Angel the landlord brought out small beer for everyone, and Jamie thought he'd never seen such a happy gathering. He was just starting to relax when Anthony said, 'Right, off we go again.'

To Jamie's amazement, and horror, the dance was repeated – all the way round the town, in and out of the houses. But this time some of the dancers were dressed in smart clothes, the Mayor and Mayoress were the top couple, and Jamie understood they were all the wealthy townsfolk. At the end they all danced straight into the Angel. In the ballroom, the dance spiralled into the centre of the room and then, with much hilarity, turned back on itself, until the dancers were eventually spread around the edge of the room and gratefully sat down.

JOSEPH EMIDY

There was a pause in the dancing as refreshments were provided. Jamie was munching an apple when other musicians entered. The first was another fiddler. Jamie's eyes opened wide – he had never seen such a man before. The new fiddler's skin was black, and Jamie was stunned into silence. The musician looked around the room, then spying Anthony James with his fiddle, walked straight to him.

'Good afternoon sir,' he said, 'Joseph Emidy is my name.'

'Anthony James, sir', said Anthony, holding out his hand. After an instant's hesitation Emidy realised that Anthony could not see, and warmly took his hand and shook it.

'Mr James…' he began.

'Joseph, please call me Anthony.'

'I have been employed to help with the music for the evening dance. I hope you don't mind.'

'Not at all, but what do you play?' asked Anthony.

'The violin, of course', said Emidy, holding up his violin case. 'Oh, I'm sorry. I quite forgot your eyes.'

'That's no bother,' said Anthony James, 'but can you play the violin?'

Joseph Emidy took out his fiddle and placed it under his chin. As his bow caressed the strings the most wonderful sound echoed across the room. As the notes leaped and soared all conversation ceased. When the music ended there was spontaneous applause. Anthony James held out his hand again; there were tears in his eyes.

'Joseph Emidy,' he said, 'you are a musician as well as a gentle-man.'

'But he's black,' said Jamie, 'he's different.'

'I can't see that', countered Anthony. 'What colour is his music? What colour are his manners?'

Emidy smiled. 'Young Jamie,' he said, 'you may have never seen a black man before. But in Falmouth they think nothing of it. It is such a busy port these days, and there you will find men of every possible colour, just getting on with their lives. But far away there are many people like me. As with white people, some are good, some are bad. In Africa it was black people that sold me into slav-ery, white that transported me and kept me in Brazil. It was white people that set me free in Lisbon. Then it was white men again that press-ganged me and men of all colours into your navy. Finally, in Falmouth it was white people that freed me a second time and gave me a home. And here in Cornwall I must say I am treated very well, and no less than in Helston, where I found my lovely wife.'

'I would love to be able to play the violin like that,' said Jamie.

A broad smile creased Emidy's face. 'You will, Jamie, you will.' Then from his bag Emidy produced a three-quarter sized violin. 'I was once a traveller who had nothing,' said Emidy, 'then Cornwall gave me a living, a wife, a home, and acceptance for what I am and what I do. Let me give something back to Cornwall. You must play it every day, just a little. When you are too big for it, give it to someone else who needs it.' He pressed the fiddle into Jamie's hands. The lad was speechless. A tear fell from Anthony's cheek.

'What do you say Jamie?' questioned Anthony.

'Thank you, Mr Emidy', said Jamie, overawed.

'Is it a magic violin?' he continued.

'All violins are magic,' said Emidy, 'but you have to be the magician.'

'I will practise,' said Jamie, 'I promise.'

Anthony James followed Emidy's eloquence by placing his fiddle under his chin.

'Emidy,' he commanded, 'it's time to strike sound!'

Then followed dance after country dance. Sometimes the fiddlers played alternately. Often their repertoire coincided and they played together, each man smiling in turn as he heard little variations or decorations from the other. Sometimes they improvised harmonies or counter melodies. When the dancers were looking weary, Anthony said, 'Time for the Triumph I think, that's the way they finish the evening these days. I learned it from John Old, the harper up at Par.'

So, with the Triumph country dance the evening ended. Farewells were said, and said again. Joseph Emidy shook Jamie's hand, and the lad looked at him with new respect. In the moonlight the dancers drifted home, two by two.

'That,' said Anthony James, 'is how Cornwall welcomes the summer.'

4

PENGERSEK

The next morning started with ten minutes practise on the violin for Jamie. Anthony, although self-taught, proved to be a patient and encouraging teacher. He thought the sound of young Jamie scraping the fiddle was the sweetest sound in the world! From then on Jamie played whenever they rested, at lunch and in the evenings. Somehow music seemed part of the scenery, and soon Jamie was joining in simple tunes. After practise was over they left Helston and crossed a deep valley with a lake in it.

'It's called the Loe Pool', said Anthony. 'I'll tell you about it another day, it's all part of a long story!' They travelled west, and as the road drew closer to the sea a tower came into view. 'That's Pengersek Castle', said Anthony. 'The people there are good, and cultured too. I have heard music from the windows. But the place has an amazing history.'

THE LEGEND OF PENGERSEK

One old lord of Pengersek went to the Crusades. While he was in those foreign lands he courted a beautiful princess and soon she was expecting his child. She loaned Pengersek a magic sword that belonged to her father. Its magic meant that its owner could never be killed in battle, but it didn't stop Pengersek from being defeated. With the magic sword still in his scabbard, Pengersek fled back to Cornwall, but he promised his princess that he would return. She took a ring from her finger and broke it in half. She gave him one half and said, 'Keep this to remember your love in a far country.' Pengersek took the broken token and he swore to be faithful to his princess.

But when old Pengersek got back Cornwall, he completely ignored his promise. He courted and married a lady from Helston and soon she had a child by him. But not much later there was a knock on the door and there stood his Eastern lover, also with a baby. Pengersek went outside, not wanting anyone in the house to hear. He told his princess that he was married and that she should return to her own land. But then she explained that she had no land to return to. She too had been defeated in battle, because Pengersek had kept the magic sword. Tyrants now ruled her country.

Pengersek pretended to be sympathetic. But as he walked with this lady, the lord ensured that their path was by the cliff edge, and there he threw her into the sea. That very day her lifeless body was found floating in the waves by the crew of a ship bound for Marazion to trade for tin. But the little baby was still alive, fast asleep in its mother's arms. That night, in a dream, a white hare appeared to the captain of the ship. The hare explained that the child's mother was a princess from the captain's own country and the child's father was the treacherous Pengersek. So the kindly sea captain decided to raise the child as his own. He brought the lad up well, but he never told him who his true parents were.

The next day Pengersek was out hunting. He was up on Tregonning Hill when a great storm engulfed him. In the midst of the storm he saw a white hare with eyes like fiery coals. In his heart Pengersek knew it was the spirit of his dead mistress. The hare so startled his horse that it reared up. Pengersek was thrown to the ground and knocked senseless. Next day he was found on the hill in a terrible state. But his scabbard was empty and, try as they might, no one could find the magic sword.

From that day Pengersek was terrified. He would not go out unless he had a priest beside him. But even so, whenever he ventured out the white hare would appear and leave him quaking with fear. The priest tried to exorcise this ghost, but found he had no power over it. Then she appeared in her human form, explaining that she was no evil spirit, but a cruelly wronged woman and she would not cease until her son received his rightful inheritance.

Old Pengersek was cruel to his Cornish wife as well, and the poor lady died young, leaving her son Marek to be raised by a nurse.

Now many years later, when Marek was a young man, he was walking by the sea when he found a poor half-drowned sailor in the water. Marek took the poor chap home to recover. The sailor's name was Arluth; he had fallen from the rigging of a ship bound for Marazion to trade for tin. So next day they set out for Marazion to reunite the sailor and his ship. As they rode along, a white doe started from a thicket and ran towards the high ground. They followed it up onto Tregonning Hill. Then from the clouds came a flash of lightning that struck the rocks ahead and split them asunder. A white hare appeared between the rocks, looked at the sailor lovingly and then disappeared. Arluth ran up to the rocks and there, where the rock was split, he found a fine sword with jewels in its hilt and a blade that shone like flame.

Arluth was delighted at this good luck. Marek too was amazed, for old Pengersek had told him nothing about his past, or about the sword that was lost. But then the two young men continued to Marazion and there they found Arluth's ship. The captain was overjoyed to see Arluth return.

'I thought you must have drowned,' said the captain, 'and I knew that your mother would never have forgiven me.' But when Arluth told him of his rescue by the heir of Pengersek and the finding of the sword, a smile spread across the captain's face. The captain explained that although he had raised Arluth, the lad's mother had been a princess and his father was old Pengersek himself. Arluth and Marek were brothers.

Marek had not yet come into his inheritance and longed for adventure, so he set sail alongside Arluth to explore his new-found *brother's Eastern lands. Back in his own country, Arluth produced the magic sword. With Marek, Arluth led his people to overcome the tyrants that had usurped his mother. In that distant land Marek learned many magic skills. There he celebrated his twenty-first birthday, and on that day he married a beautiful lady.*

And on that very same day, Pengersek was riding on the Marazion Road when a white hare with blazing eyes sprang out before him. Pengersek's horse turned and galloped straight into the sea. The horse and its rider were never seen again. A messenger was sent from Cornwall to tell Marek that old Pengersek was dead and that he had come into his inheritance.

So Marek and his bride sailed home. When they returned there was the greatest feast that had ever been at Pengersek. From that day onwards Marek's bride would play her harp in one of the castle towers. The music was so beautiful that passing fishermen would rest on their oars and seabirds would come to listen to the music.

So, at last, peace came to Pengersek. But on dark nights you can still see the ghost of Marek up in his tower, using the skills he learned in the East to raise magic fire, and with it gazing into the future, the past and lands that are far away.

5

MARAZION

After Pengersek the road wound ever closer to the shining sea.

'Let me know when you see something!' said Anthony.

'What? See what?' questioned the lad.

'You'll know when you see it', was the enigmatic reply.

The sun was high in the sky when Jamie called out, 'I can see it!'

'What can you see?' asked Anthony.

'A castle. A proper fairytale castle on an island; and there's a path to it under the sea.'

The castle and the rock on which it stood were both of a light-coloured stone that gleamed in the sun. Where rock ended and castle began was not easy to determine. The shallow sea covered a causeway that led to the island from the small town on the mainland opposite. Jamie saw there was a well-protected little harbour below the castle on the landward side of the island.

'They used to export the tin from there, even back in Roman times', said Anthony. 'When the tide's out, the causeway is how the tinners take their carts and pack horses and carry the tin out to the island. And though it's pretty enough, that's no fairytale castle; it's for real. In the Civil War it held out against the Roundheads for years. The rocky island is called St Michael's Mount.'

'St Michael?' asked Jamie thoughtfully, 'The archangel?'

'The very man', said Anthony. 'God's chief warrior! If you go to

Bodmin they say the saint of Cornwall is St Petroc. If you ask a tin miner, he will say St Piran, for he is indeed the patron saint of tinners. But in these parts they say that St Michael is the patron saint of Cornwall.'

ST MICHAEL AND THE MOUNT

The Devil wanted Cornwall for himself. But like some people I know he couldn't keep a secret, so he told one of his imps. But that imp couldn't keep a secret either, so he told a goblin. But that goblin couldn't keep a secret either… and so it went on and on. Eventually St Michael himself got to hear of the Devil's ambition. So the archangel set up camp on the rocky island we now call St Michael's Mount. Every day he would sit on a special seat in the rocks called St Michael's Chair. From there he could watch over the fishermen in Mount's Bay, and from there he could spy the Devil if ever he should come near.

Well, one day St Michael was looking out and in the east he saw a great fire-breathing dragon. It was flying directly towards Cornwall. Straight away St Michael realised that its soul had been possessed by none other than Old Nick, Old Scratch, the Devil himself. In its claws the dragon held a great, red-hot boulder taken straight from the fires of hell. The hell stone, it was called, and the dragon intended to drop it and destroy the very town and people we visited only yesterday. So St Michael flew up into the sky. In his hand was a sword made of pure fire. In turn, the dragon breathed fire back at St Michael. But the dragon couldn't use its talons because they were holding onto the hell stone. St Michael struck the dragon a mighty blow with his sword and the dragon let go of the red-hot stone. Through the sky the stone tumbled. It could have been fatal, but as the stone fell St Michael shouted a warning. 'Stand from under!' he cried. In the town below the people scattered and the stone landed right behind the Angel Hotel. When it cooled down the hell stone was a great black boulder, and the town has been called Helston ever since. The stone was in the yard behind the Angel until just the other year, then someone broke it up to build a wall.

But although the dragon dropped the stone, it was too late to save itself. With his sword of fire St Michael struck the dragon another great blow, and it fell out of the sky into the Loe Pool, just south of Helston, and it has never been seen again.

But good old St Michael, he still keeps a friendly eye out for Cornwall, and for Cornish fishermen in particular. Years ago some fishermen were making their way back into Mount's Bay. But then the mist came down; it was so thick you could almost lean on it. The fishermen didn't know which way to go at all. They could easily have finished up on the rocks and been drowned. Then they heard a voice calling out, so they followed it. Sure enough, there was St Michael up on his seat on top of the Mount, pointing the way back to harbour. So in Bodmin they have Petroc, the tinners have Piran, but in these parts they will always tell you that St Michael is their patron saint, and for good reason too!

As they grew closer the Mount seemed so close you could almost reach out and touch it. Jamie could now clearly see the little harbour on the island. 'That's the main harbour hereabouts,' said Anthony, 'though I do hear they are talking of building a big new harbour at Penzance.'

Shortly they entered the small town opposite the Mount.

'Marazion,' announced Anthony, 'it means "little market".' Street traders vied with each other, and crowds filled the roadway. All around was hustle and bustle, talk and laughter. 'But today's Thursday,' said Anthony James, 'market day; that means it's time I earned us a crust or two.' Soon many people gathered around, intrigued by Anthony's riddles and amused by his songs. 'Let the horse stroke the cat; hear the wood sing,' cried Anthony. Then he self-consciously took up his violin and played it, and gradually there was a smile of understanding from the crowd.

'I'll tell you a story,' cried Anthony, and there was a murmur of assent. Children gathered at his feet. Their parents stood behind them, but listened just as attentively. Anthony scanned the crowd with his sightless eyes. The people fell quiet and he started to speak.

JACK THE GIANT-KILLER

Once upon a time, in Cornwall there was a huge giant called Cormoran. He lived in a cave at the top of St Michael's Mount and he was the terror of all the countryside.

Now Cormoran was three times as tall as the tallest man, and his waist was so big that it took ten minutes to walk round him. He had red hair with worms in it, and great goggling eyes, and when he walked the earth shook as if there was an earthquake.

Now this giant was always hungry and every day he waded from the Mount to the mainland. He raided the farms round Marazion for animals to eat. Sometimes he would take half a dozen cows and sling them over his shoulder. Sometimes he would take a dozen sheep, and tuck them into his belt. Then he would wade home, gobble them up, and start to feel hungry again.

No one dared face Cormoran and try to stop him. He was so big that everyone ran away in terror when they felt the ground tremble. He never paid for what he took and he never, ever, said please or thank you.

But living near Marazion was a farmer's son named Jack. He saw how the good people round about him worked from dawn to dusk, only to starve when their sheep and cattle were stolen by Cormoran. Jack grew more and more upset each time that Cormoran came and carried off the animals, for each time another family had to go hungry.

'It is time this monster was punished,' said Jack, 'and as no one else will do it, it will have to be me.'

So from his father's shed Jack took a shovel and a pickaxe, and from the coachman he borrowed a horn, and that evening he went across to the Mount. The giant was asleep in his cave. Jack took the shovel and started to dig. All night long he dug and dug until he had made a deep hole at the foot of the Mount. Then Jack carefully covered over the hole with long sticks and straw, and then he spread earth and bracken on the top so that it looked like solid ground.

By this time it was nearly dawn, but the giant was still fast asleep. Then Jack picked up the coachman's horn and blew it as loud as he could. At once there was a howl of rage from inside the cave. 'Who dares make such an awful noise and wake me up?' Cormoran shouted. The giant appeared in the mouth of the cave and soon the earth began to shake as he came stamping down the hill. Then he saw Jack, and he shook with rage, and his goggling eyes flashed fire.

'You miserable little shrimp, I'll teach you to disturb me!' shouted the giant. 'I will boil you like an egg for my breakfast!' He reached out his hairy hand and was just about to seize Jack around the middle.

The giant's fingers were an inch from Jack's waist. But Jack was standing on the other side of the covered hole. Just before old Cormoran could touch him, the straw and sticks gave way, and the giant tumbled headlong into the trap.

'Aha!' said Jack, 'Boil me for breakfast, would you?'

The giant struggled to his feet in the bottom of the pit and as his head appeared just above the ground, Jack took his pickaxe and with a mighty swing brought it down on the Cormoran's head and killed him on the spot.

When the people of Cornwall heard the giant was dead they were very grateful. At last, they could live in peace and not have the fruits of their labours stolen by someone whose only attributes were greed, strength and bad manners. They declared that Jack should be known throughout the land as Jack the Giant-Killer. They made him a splendid belt, on which was embroidered in golden letters, 'This is the

valiant Cornishman, who slew the Giant Cormoran.'

Jack's fame soon spread all over the countryside, and every other giant who heard of him vowed vengeance against Jack the Giant-Killer. So Jack had many more adventures, but that, as they say, is another story. But, friends, before you go on your way, just remember the most famous line in that story should always be, 'Fe-, fi-, fo-, fum, I smell the blood of a Cornishman!'

There was laughter and applause from the crowd. Jamie took the hat round and soon it was jingling with coins. Then they both sat down to eat together.

Anthony said, 'Now that was what they all like to hear! But there is more to that story.'

'Really?' asked Jamie, so Anthony continued.

CORMORAN AND CORMELIAN

When Cormoran was young he had a wife, a lady giant called Cormelian, who lived with him on St Michael's Mount. She cooked for him, looked after him, kept his house in order and made sure he minded his manners. Even though they were not well-off they were happy and Cormoran was quite pleasant as giants go.

Now, Cormoran was very friendly with another giant, Trecrobben, a cousin of his who lived over by Trencrom, about three miles further north. These two giants had just one cobbling-hammer between them. This they would throw back and forth between St Michaels Mount and Trencrom when either of them happened to need it. One afternoon Cormoran looked at his boots and he saw one had a great hole in it. It needed new leather cutting and nailing in place. So he cut the leather, but then he found that Trecrobben had the hammer. So he called out from the mouth of his cave, 'Hallo, Trecrobben, throw us down the hammer.' 'Certainly, but you make sure you catch it,' answered Trecrobben.

Now Trecrobben was a fine figure of a giant, and Cormelian rather enjoyed watching Trecrobben's athletics. Also, she wanted to ask after Mrs Trecrobben and get the latest gossip from the hills to the north. So Cormelian came stumbling out of her dark cave into the bright sunlight, which dazzled her eyes. Before she could shade her face with her apron, she barged into her husband so he couldn't catch the hammer. Then down came the hammer and hit Cormelian right between the eyes, and she fell stone dead on the ground. It was the most terrible accident. They buried her deep under the Mount, and the noise that the giants made when mourning the giantess was terrible – it echoed from hill to hill all across Cornwall.

Old Trecrobben buried his treasure deep among the cairns of his castle, and then he grieved himself to death because he felt responsible for killing his old friend's wife. On moonlit nights many people have dug by the cairns up on Trencrom in hopes of finding his crocks of gold. But whenever they get deep enough to touch the flat stone that covers the mouth of a crock, and hear it ring hollow, out from the crevices of the rocks and cairns come hordes of spriggans. They cause storms and thunder and lightning, and they always scare the diggers away.

Also from that day Cormoran got more and more bad tempered. He had no one to look after him or make sure he minded his manners. It was then that he took to pleasing himself in a most selfish way, which was quite unfair to all the people round about. That, of course is where the story of Jack the Giant-Killer begins.

Jamie said, 'That's a bit sad. Couldn't Jack have just warned the giant not to do it again, or locked him up?'

Anthony smiled grimly. 'It might have been worth a try; he might have turned over a new leaf' he said. 'But some people just won't be told, dictators and the like. It's never an easy decision, but sometimes you just have to look after yourself.'

6

LUDGVAN

Next day the two travellers left Marazion heading west. For most of the time they walked beside the sea. Mount's Bay was dotted with fishing boats. As they walked they talked.

'What colour is the sand?' asked Anthony.

'Well,' said Jamie, 'by the Mount and by the river it's... it's black. Then ahead of us it's yellow.'

'I thought I remembered that', said Anthony. 'The black sand is tiny pieces of tin ore. They used to stream for tin in the river here, just like gold prospectors do. Out by the Mount they've been loading ships with tin for nearly two thousand years, so it's not surprising that the sand is that colour.'

'Can you count?' asked Anthony.

'One, two, three, four, five... I can get to a hundred', said Jamie.

'Good. Do you know how fishermen count?' asked Anthony again.

'I think so, the long-liners from Mullion taught me', said Jamie.

'Go on then.'

'Onan, dew, trei, pajar, pemp... I can get to twenty, and I can say the "Our Father" in Cornish too.'

'Ha!' snorted Anthony, 'But well done. There are precious few who can still do that. The old language is nearly dead. Many don't realise that Cornwall has it own language, nothing at all like English.'

'You say something,' challenged the boy. Anthony smiled.

'Dedh da', said Anthony, slowly.[1]

'Dedh da', repeated Jamie. 'What does it mean?'

'It means "good day". "Dedh" means day, and "da" means good',
said Anthony.

'Tell me Jamie,' he continued, 'are there fishing boats in the
bay?'

'There are', said Jamie. 'Nothing bigger though.'

'Good', said Anthony, breathing a sigh of relief. 'Here lad, what
do you make of this?':

A mi a moaz, a mi a moaz in Goon Glaze,

Mi a clouaz, a clouaz, a clouaz, a troz, a troz, a troz, an pysgaz miniz.

Bez mi a trouviaz un pysg brawze, naw losia,

Olla boble en Porthia ha Marazjowan

Ne mi ôr dho gan zingy.

Jamie looked blank, so Anthony translated for him:

As I was going, as I was going on a blue plain

I heard, I heard, I heard, the sound, the sound, the sound, of little
fishes.

But then I found a great fish, with nine tails,

All the people in St Ives and Marazion

Could never get hold of it.

Jamie still looked blank and Anthony continued, 'It's a riddle.
What do you think it is?'

'A whale in the sea?'

'I think the sea is right. But how many tails has a whale?'

'Is it an octopus?'

'Not enough legs,' said Anthony, 'an octopus has eight, but the
riddle says nine tails.'

'I give up,' said Jamie.

Anthony looked conspiratorial. 'It's a secret message,' he said, 'to
the Cornish fishermen from Mount's Bay. The fish with nine tails

is the cat o' nine tails, used by the navy to discipline sailors. It's a warning to Cornish-speaking fishermen of the English press gang. So if you see anyone in uniform, you tell me.'

Jamie looked unconvinced. 'I'm too young,' he said. There was an awkward pause before he continued, 'and they wouldn't take you, not now.'

Anthony grimaced, 'You're right lad. But old habits die hard. The King's had me once; he's not having me again. Can you still see St Michael's Mount?'

THE LEGEND OF LYONESSE

In about 1600 St Michael's Mount was called 'carreck loces in cowse'; it means 'the grey rock in the wood' in Cornish. Now, the St Michael's Mount that we know is an island, surrounded by the sea for much of the time. But when the tide is very low you can see old tree stumps sticking up out of the sand. That's because things were different long ago. Once there was a scholar called William of Worcester. He came to Cornwall in the fifteenth century; he heard this tale and he wrote it down.

Many years ago the water level was much lower than it is today and there was a great land west of Cornwall. The Cornish called it Lethowstow, but now we know it as Lyonesse. Its most famous King was Tristan. The capital was called the City of Lions. There were a hundred and forty parishes, with churches, towns, villages and fields. It stretched far to the west, with a watchtower at the farthest point to guide sailors.

But one day, and some say it was in 1099, there came the greatest storm that ever there was. The great waves broke down the sea defences and the water came rushing in across the fields. All of Lyonesse was submerged and only one man escaped. His name was Trevillian; he came from Basil, near Launceston. Some people say he was one of King Arthur's knights! When Trevillian saw the waves approaching he leapt on his milk-white steed. There was no time to put on a saddle and bareback he galloped ahead of the waves. But the racing tide was faster than even the swiftest horse. Soon the water was lapping at the horse's heels. Then the horse was splashing through shallow water. For a perilous moment the horse stumbled as the great waves swept it off its feet. Trevillian held on tight with his hands and his heels. After what seemed like minutes, but can only have been seconds, the horse found itself swimming towards the shore. Patiently it swam, then its feet touched bottom and it was able to walk to safety. So it was that Trevillian was the only man to escape the drowning of Lyonesse. His successors, the Trevelyans, live on to this day.

The fishermen say they still bring up bits of doors and window frames in their nets, especially in the area they call Tregva, out by the Seven Stones reef. They say that if you hear the bells of Lyonesse ringing, then another great storm is on the way.

'Crumbs,' said Jamie, looking at the sea with a new respect, just in case it should be thinking of another inundation.

Soon there was a village before them. Right beside the church of St Ludgvan was an inn, the White Hart. It was warm and cosy, every snug had a fire. The landlady smiled at Jamie. As Anthony played and sang she brought them food and drink. The local people too seemed kindly. They joined in the songs and sang others themselves. The songs were all in English, Jamie noted.

That night Anthony and Jamie slept by the fire, but with warm blankets provided by the motherly landlady. Jamie slept soundly until he woke with a start in the middle of the night. 'No, no, no!' he was calling out.

'What is it Jamie?' said Anthony, holding the lad close. 'You must have been dreaming.'

'I just heard an awful sound,' said Jamie, 'a wild animal, baying, crying, calling, weeping... It was as if it had lost its mate and was calling out in despair, one final time.'

'My God,' said Anthony James, 'it's the wolf. The echoes are still here.'

THE LAST WOLF

The last wolf in Cornwall, perhaps the last in the British Isles, lived in the forests of Ludgvan, near Penzance. It was a huge animal; local people say it caused terrible havoc with their flocks of sheep. Tradition says that at last the wolf carried off a child, so the people all turned out and this famous wolf was captured at a place now called Rospeath, just half a mile south-east of Crowlas. It means 'heath of the wolf' in Cornish. Most people think Ludgvan was a little-known saint after whom the church and village were named. But others suggest he was not a saint at all, but a great warrior that killed the wolf.

But I have a different idea. I think the wolf was killed because people were frightened. Most had never met a wolf, but they had heard that wolves were dangerous: part of a different, unknown world. But this wolf was wise. It knew all the old ways, the secrets of the past. The wolf offered those secrets to the hunters. It said, 'I am different to you, but you do not need to hunt me. Like you, I am mortal. Soon my days on this earth will be done, but in the meantime I can teach you much.' But the hunters cared nothing for what the wolf could teach them. They were more concerned with the wolf's reputation, rather than what it was really like. So instead of learning from it they destroyed it. Now, like the language of my father, it's gone. But its cries still echo across the land. Only the right people can hear it, the blessed or the cursed.

'Which am I, Anthony?' asked Jamie. 'Which am I?'

Notes

1   In Standard Written Form Cornish, 'dh' sounds as the letters 'th' in the English word 'the'.

7

Seyth

PENZANCE

Next day Anthony James and young Jamie walked into Penzance. The road was busy, and it was clear that the flourishing tin industry was bringing a new prosperity to the town. The broad main street was flanked by grand houses. There was talk of a great new harbour to export the tin ore for smelting and import the coal needed for steam engines. Everyone seemed in a hurry, and not at all interested in tunes or tales. Somehow folk tunes and fireside tales seemed part of a world that at least some of the locals wished to leave behind. Anthony listened to the hustle and bustle of the town. Then he spoke.

'A long time ago there was just one man lived here. He was a holy man who built his house on the headland. There he could gather shellfish, do a little fishing and find peace with his God. That's why they called the promontory the "holy headland". "Penn" means head; "sans" means holy. Now they still call it Penzance, but it is very different these days. It's strange, there's all this new wealth with the tin mining and the trading, but there still seem to be lots of poor people in this world.'

In the inn, fishermen spoke words that Jamie could not understand. 'That's more Cornish', said Anthony. 'As well as counting, the fishermen name the parts of the boat and give their sailing instructions in Cornish. And they pray in Cornish too. Not that they are particularly religious, but they are superstitious.'

'What does that mean?' asked Jamie.

'They believe in signs and seasons,' said Anthony, 'like it says in the book of Genesis. "God said, Let there be lights in the firmament of the heaven to divide the day from the night; and let them be for signs, and for seasons." They believe in mermaids and sea monsters, and all manner of things. There's supposed to be a sea monster off Falmouth Bay, Morgawr they call it.'

Next they met an old farmer from New Mill, a poor hamlet north-west of the town. He spoke little English and dolefully he recited these garbled words:

A grankan, a grankan,
A mean o gowaz o vean
Ondez parc an venton
Dub trelowza vean
Far Penzans a Maragow
Githack mackwee
A githack macrow
A mac trelowza varrack.

'My Cornish isn't good enough. What does it mean?' whispered Jamie.

'It's not you,' said Anthony James, 'his words are confusing. But I suppose it's a complaint. Grankan is a farm just this side of New Mill. The poet that wrote those words was literally saying that the fields at Grankan are barren compared with the road between Penzance and Marazion. But figuratively he meant that the traditional farming life is poorly rewarded compared to that of the merchants and traders of the town.'

O Grankan, O Grankan!
Beyond the fields of the spring
you give but little
– only three shoots by the stone.

The road between Penzance and Marazion
is very green
and much fresher:
three shoots grow for every passing horseman.

'He is probably right too. Old Billy Foss has a rhyme with much
the same sentiment, about the pastures of Boslow, up in the hills
behind St Just.'

No grass for the flocks,
But a carn of dry rocks,
Which afforded a horrible sight;
If you chance go that way,
You must do so by day,
For you'd smash out your brains in the night!

A sad, bent figure in the corner spoke out. 'The world is changing,
son.' The speaker shuffled towards them with an uneven gait. As
he came into the light, Jamie could see a hand-bell hanging at his
waist. From the crook of one arm hung a wicker basket containing
printed sheets of poetry, weighed down with a large black book.
He seized a sheet and read:

Our Cornish drolls are dead, each one;
The fairies from their haunts have gone:
There's scarce a witch in all the land,
The world has grown so learn'd and grand.

'Aha!' said Anthony James, '"Henny" Quick, the poet of Zennor!'

'At your service', said Henry, gloomily. 'Of Zennor, and late of
Penzance gaol! Boase the Mayor objects to me ringing my bell and
declaiming my poetry. I've not earned a penny.'

'I do agree that times are changing,' said
Anthony, 'but I hope you're wrong about the
drolls. For what doesn't change is our need to earn
a few pence! We must try and prove you wrong!'

Henry called out 'Good luck!' as the two of them left the inn and walked into the road outside. The street was called Market Jew Street.

'Are there lots of Jews here?' asked Jamie.

'There are some,' said Anthony, 'but they live up in Leskinnick Terrace, so they have nothing to do with the name of this street! This is the road to Marazion, where the market is on Thursdays. Thursday Market is "Marhas Yow" in Cornish. But people who didn't know the language wrote it down as Market Jew! So it's nothing to do with religion and all to do with geography and language!'

Though the street was grand it proved impossible to drum up trade for tunes or tales. No one seemed to have time to listen. Anthony took from his bag some folded papers with ballads printed on them.

'Only a penny. Read the tragedy of "Crantock Games"; laugh at "Richard of Taunton Dean".'

They hadn't sold a single broadside when a voice cried out, 'There, more vagabonds, lock them up. Take them to the beak!' Two constables seized them, and even though Anthony was blind and Jamie diminutive, they were roughly manhandled into a dark cell. Anthony was shaken and trembled with fear. Jamie was angry, if subdued. After what seemed an age they were led to a large room. There sat a large man in a suit. At his side were the two constables. Jamie heard the word 'vagabond' repeated as the constables spoke with the seated man. Then suddenly he stood and spoke.

'People say you are itinerants and vagabonds. We don't want such people in Penzance. What have you to say for yourself?' Jamie looked at Anthony. The old soldier could not speak, but was trembling with fear or anger, Jamie could not tell which. Then Jamie summoned up all his courage.

'If you please Sir,' he said, 'I will speak, as Mr James is not well.'

'Shut up, Jamie,' whispered Anthony, 'that's Henry Boase the Mayor, he'll lock us up.'

'Please, Mr Boase,' said Jamie, 'We do no harm. Mr James is blind and I am his guide. We play music, sing songs and tell stories.

Usually people laugh and dance and are happy to see us. We are very sorry if people are not happy, for people only pay us after we have performed, for we owe no one anything.'

There was a moment's silence. One of the constables started to shout but Boase turned and silenced him.

'Well spoken, young man,' said Boase, 'that was a brave thing to do. But what does the old blind crowder have to say for himself?'

Anthony James stood erect. Jamie had never seen him look so tall. 'The reason I am an old blind fiddler is because, as you can tell from my clothes, I fought for the King, for you and for all the people of this land, and in doing so I lost my sight. The King is grateful and kindly provides my winter quarters, but in the warmer months I fend for myself. I do so honestly. As I'm sure you can imagine, a blind man makes a poor thief.'

'Very well,' said Boase, 'this is how it will be. Go, hawk your broadsides, sing your songs, bring some laughter to the town. But you leave tomorrow morning at dawn. If you do not do so, I will lock you up without fail.'

The front door was opened and through it Jamie saw the street. 'Thank you, sir,' said Jamie, though he was not sure if he meant it, and he led Anthony into the sunshine.

8

Eth

MOUSEHOLE

As instructed, Anthony and Jamie left Penzance early next day and made their way through Newlyn. It seemed worlds away from the bustle of the port they had just left. Bearded old fishermen mended their nets by the quay and Jamie imagined they had been there for hundreds of years. The same was true of Mousehole, the next cove, only a couple of miles along the coast.

There Jamie described the scene to Anthony. Anthony explained that originally there were two hamlets, one either side of the stream, but they shared the little harbour. The entrance to the harbour was so small the fishermen called it the Mousehole, pronounced 'Mouzel'. Then the harbour was called Mousehole, and eventually the village grew and it was called Mousehole too.

TOM BAWCOCK

One winter, the storms were the worst anyone in Cornwall had ever known. The narrow entrance to the little harbour which the fishermen called the Mousehole was impassable. Great breakers swept across it, and out at sea the waves were big enough to overwhelm any ship. It was nearly Christmas, but no one had been able to go fishing for weeks, and the people of Mousehole were starving.

In those days a fisherman called Tom Bawcock lived in Mousehole. He was a good seaman, as are most Cornish fishermen. On the day before Christmas Eve, Tom Bawcock decided he would take a chance. He thought it was better to risk drowning while trying to catch something than just starving to death doing nothing.

So Tom summoned up his courage. On his mast he set the smallest sail he could. Picking his moment he sailed boldly out through the Mousehole just as one great wave passed. Then he bore away to gain both steerage way and sea room before the next wave arrived. He only had a pocket handkerchief for a sail, but the wind was so strong that he struggled to keep his boat upright and under control. But somehow he made his way to windward, dodging the breakers. From the leeward rail he trailed seven long lines, all hooked and baited. Then, when he had sailed as far as he dared, he hove to and pulled in the lines. On each line was a different sort of fish. There were morgi (dog fish, that is), lances (sand eels), fair maids (pilchards), ling (a sort of cod), hake, scad and mackerel!

So Tom tacked round and sailed back to Mousehole. He headed up to windward of the entrance and then sailed in as if he were racing. As he came rushing in the biggest wave you can imagine picked him up, carried him down to leeward and he came flying in through the harbour entrance.

Back at Mousehole everyone came out to cheer old Tom. The fisher-lasses took the seven sorts of fish, and made them into a great fish and potato pie. To decorate it the fish heads were left sticking out of the middle and the tails were left sticking out of the edge of the crust, so it was called a Starry Gazey Pie. So it was that the village of Mousehole was saved. Since that day in Mousehole they celebrate 23 December as Tom Bawcock's Eve, and they always eat Starry Gazey Pie.

THE PROPHECY OF MERLIN

Off the southern end of Mousehole quay is a rock called Merlin's Rock. The old magician knew Cornwall well, and once he pointed out that rock and made what people call 'The Prophecy of Merlin'. It goes like this:

> Ewra teyre a war meane Merlyn,
> Ara lesky Pawle, Pensanz ha Newlyn.

Translated:

> There shall land on the Rock of Merlin
> Those who shall burn Paul, Penzance and Newlyn.

His prophecy was right, for in 1595 four Spanish galleons did come and they did exactly what Merlin said. The Royal Navy was nowhere to be seen and the local militia was overwhelmed. The Spanish came ashore at Mousehole and ransacked and burned the towns of Mount's Bay.

But they were deterred from attacking Penryn because when they reached the town, there a play was being performed. The climax of the play was a battle scene in which cannons and muskets were fired. When the Spanish heard the guns being fired they thought the redcoats had arrived and so they fled back out to sea. It must have been a very impressive play!

The next place the Spanish went was Padstow. But that, as they say, is another story.

9

Naω

St Buryan

After Mousehole they headed inland. Ahead, old standing stones and a stone circle could be seen. There was a church tower on the horizon. Soon they reached a lane leading to an old manor. Jamie read the name, 'Trewoofe'.

'Ah yes,' said Anthony, '"Trove" is how they say it round here. This is another tale I heard from Billy Foss.'

DUFFY AND THE DEVIL

One autumn, when it was cider-making time, Squire Lovel of Trove rode up to Buryan to hire young men and women, some to pick the apples from his trees, others to carry them to the cider mill.

But as the Squire arrived he heard shouting and scolding. Old Janey Chygwin was beating her step-daughter Duffy about the head with the skirt of her swing-tail gown. Janey had been using the skirt-tail to carry the ashes and there was so much dust that the Squire was nearly choked and blinded.

'What's the matter, Janey?' cried the Squire.

'This lazy hussy!' shouted Janey, 'She spends all her time with the boys! She never stays in to boil the porridge, knit the stockings or spin the yarn.'

'Don't believe her, Squire,' said Duffy, 'my knitting and spinning are the best in the parish.'

Now Duffy was a very pretty young lady and the Squire decided to take Duffy home with him to do the spinning.

'But she's useless!' shouted old Janey.

'Why not try me,' said Duffy, curtsying very low, 'my yarns are the very best.'

'Janey will be glad to get rid of you,' said the Squire; 'and you will be pleased to leave her; so jump up behind me, Duffy!'

No sooner said than done! Duffy, quite shameless, jumped up on the horse behind the Squire and they jogged down to Trove.

The housekeeper took Duffy up to the garret where the wool was kept and where the spinning was done in the summer. There she asked Duffy to start work. But the truth was that Duffy was lazy and could neither knit nor spin. Now she had to do both! The garret was piled from the floor to the roof with fleeces of wool. Duffy looked at them in despair, and then sat down at the spinning-wheel and cried out, 'Curse the spinning and knitting! The Devil may spin and knit for the Squire for all I care.' As soon as Duffy said these words she heard a noise behind the woolpacks and out came a funny-looking little man. His eyes sent out flashes of light. There was something very knowing in the twist of his mouth and his curved nose had an air of intelligence. He was dressed in black and came towards Duffy with a jaunty air.

'Duffy dear,' said the little man, 'I will spin and knit for thee.'

'Thank you', said Duffy, amazed.

'Duffy dear, a lady you shall be.'

'Thank you indeed!' said Duffy.

'But, Duffy dear, for me to play your game, after three years you're mine, unless you find my name.'

Duffy was not frightened, nor did she hesitate, but struck the bargain with her devilish friend. In return he said she had only to wish and it would be granted. As for the spinning and knitting, she would find all she needed under the black ram's fleece. Then in an instant the little man vanished.

Duffy idly sang a song, and then slept until it was time for her to appear. Then she wished for some yarns, and looking under the black fleece she found them. The housekeeper showed them to the Squire, and both declared they had never seen such beautiful spinning.

The next day Duffy had to knit this yarn into stockings. Duffy idled, as only expert idlers can, and then slept until it was time to appear. Then she wished for some stockings, and under the black fleece she found them. They were as fine as silk and as strong as leather. Squire Lovel gave them a trial, and declared he would never wear any other than Duffy's stockings. He had hunted through brake and briar, furze and brambles. There was not a scratch on his legs and he was as dry as a bone. Duffy's stockings were perfect!

Then Duffy had a rare old time. She did as she pleased and went where she wanted. She was always finding excuses to go to the mill. Sometimes the miller would play his fiddle, sometimes a crowd would beat out the rhythm, and she danced on the mill-bed or swapped stories with women who brought their grist to be ground.

Now Duffy was best friends with Old Bet, the miller's wife. But Bet noticed that though Duffy's work was always done, she was always idle. So it was that Bet guessed who did Duffy's work, but never told anyone the secret.

On Sundays the people came from miles to Buryan Church, just to see the Squire's stockings. He could hunt:

Through brambles and furze in all sorts of weather;
His old shanks were as sound as if bound up in leather.

For her beauty and her skill, Duffy was now courted by young men from miles around. So the Squire, fearing to lose a girl that was both pretty and useful, married her himself. So Duffy became Lady Lovel. She kept the Devil hard at work. Wonderful stockings, overcoats and underclothes were produced and passed off as her own. Duffy had a merry time and the Squire sported and drank and minded not at all, so long as she provided him with knitted garments.

But when the three years were nearly up, Duffy still did not know the Devil's name. She thought that she should have to go down below and became very melancholy. Old Bet was sympathetic and tried to cheer up Duffy, saying that she would help. But when Duffy went up to the garret, there was the Devil teasing her more each day and telling her of her impending fate.

Eventually there was just one day left. Duffy didn't know what to do, so at last she asked Bet to help. Bet told Duffy to bring down to the mill a bottle of the strongest beer in the Squire's cellar. She was not to go to bed until the Squire returned from hunting, no matter how late, and she was not to reply to anything the Squire might say. So Duffy took the beer to the mill, and then nervously went home to wait. No sooner had Duffy left the mill than Old Bet came out with a crowd on her shoulder and the beer in her hand. No one knew where she went.

After midnight Duffy was worried. Then at last the Squire arrived, but like a madman he kept singing, 'Here's to the Devil with his wooden pick and shovel.' He was not drunk, nor frightened, but he was wild with excitement. Eventually he said, 'Duffy, you're not smiling; but I'll tell you something to make you laugh.'

True to her orders, Duffy said not a word, and the Squire said this, 'Duffy dear, I left home at break of day and hunted from Trove to Trevidder, but I never found anything. I decided to hunt all night, just to bring something home. I hunted and hunted, and at midnight up started a fine hare. She passed the Pipers and the Standing Stones, then she dived into the Fugoe Hole. I followed, with owls and bats flying round my head. On I went, through water and mud, a mile or more. I turned a corner and there were witches in scores. Amongst them was our Bet of the Mill, with her crowd in her hand. Then the witches gathered round a fire and fanned it till it flared up in a brilliant blue flame. Then I saw a queer little man in black, with a long forked tail. Bet struck her crowd and beat up a tune:

Here's to the Devil.
With his wooden pick and shovel,
Digging tin by the bushel,
With his tail cock'd up!

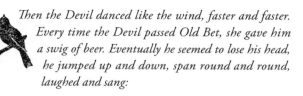

Then the Devil danced like the wind, faster and faster. Every time the Devil passed Old Bet, she gave him a swig of beer. Eventually he seemed to lose his head, he jumped up and down, span round and round, laughed and sang:

*I have knit and spun for her
Three years to the day,
To-morrow she shall ride with me,
Over land and over sea,
Far away ! Far away !
For she can never know
That my name is Tarraway!'*

When the Squire sung those lines, he saw Duffy turn pale, then red, then pale again. But she said nothing, so he continued, 'After the dance, the witches circled the fire, again they blew, again the blue flames rose. Then the Devil danced through and through the fire. It was so much fun I shouted out, "Go to it, Old Nick!" Then the lights went out, and I had to run as fast as I could, with all the witches chasing me. But I scampered safely home. Now doesn't that make you laugh, Duffy?'

Then Duffy laughed indeed, and laughed and laughed and laughed, and went happily to bed.

But when she woke she was still apprehensive. The three years were up. Had she heard the Squire correctly? Had the Squire heard the Devil correctly? Had the Devil told the truth?

Duffy had willed for a huge supply of knitted things and filled every chest in the house. She was cramming some more socks into a chest when suddenly the Devil appeared. He bowed, almost to the ground, but gave Duffy a lecherous leer. He said:

*I have worked for three years as we agreed,
So come with me, and make no objection.*

Said Duffy:

> *Your land is warm indeed.*
> *It might spoil my fair complexion.*

The Devil came closer:

> *It is not as hot as some folk say,*
> *So come with me this very day.*
> *I've kept my word; you do the same.*
> *Can you tell to me my name?*

Duffy curtsyed, and the Devil got still closer. She said:

> *You're rather close now; tell me Sir,*
> *Perhaps your name is Lucifer?*

He grinned:

> *Lucifer? What, Lucifer?*
> *That's my servant to whom you refer!*
> *You've two guesses more, for what they're worth.*
> *But my name is hardly known on Earth.*

Duffy smiled:

> *I would hate your name to snub*
> *Perhaps you're called Beelzebub?*

How the Devil laughed!

> *Beelzebub! He's just common kine.*
> *He's just a Cornish cousin of mine!*

Duffy curtsied low:

I hope your honour takes no offence.
My error is but ignorance.

The Devil danced around Duffy and was about to seize her:

My lord I beg you stop, I pray,
Perhaps your name is Tarraway!

The gentleman in black froze and stared at Duffy. She sternly looked him in the eye. 'Tarraway! Deny it if you dare', she said.

'A gentleman never denies his name,' replied Tarraway, with dignity. 'I did not expect to be beaten by a minx like you, Duffy. However, fear not, the pleasure of your company is merely postponed.' Then Tarraway vanished in a cloud of smoke, and all the Devil's knitting suddenly turned to ashes.

At that moment Squire Lovel was hunting up on the moors; the day was cold and the winds piercing. Suddenly the stockings and trousers dropped off his legs and the overcoat flew from his back. He rode home with nothing on but his shirt and his shoes. So pleased was he to get home and put on any clothes at all that he never noticed they were not very well made, and both he and Duffy lived happily ever after.

10

Deg

PORTHCURNO

The lanes took the travellers back to the coast. The rocky cliffs were very rugged. On one rocky headland a huge boulder was perched right on the edge of the cliffs.

'That's the Logan Rock', announced Anthony.

'Why is it called that?' asked Jamie.

Anthony replied, 'To "log" is an old word that means "to rock". So a logan rock is a rocking rock! On this coast there used to be many. Huge boulders weighing tons that nature left balancing so that you or I could rock them with just one hand. People used to say they were the playthings of Cornish giants. This one here was tipped onto the beach by some soldiers, but the local people made them put it back. They said if it wasn't replaced it would bring bad luck. It cost those soldiers an arm and a leg it did. You can still see the anchor holes in the rock where they attached the block and tackle to put the rock back in its place on the top of the cliff. It weighed about eighty tons.'

As if echoing the local peoples' past displeasure at the despoiling of the landscape, the sea seemed to grow wilder. Half a storm was blowing when they reached Porthcurno. There they were pleased to find a tiny kiddleywink, a cottage given over to small beer and good company. The afternoon was dark and cloudy and it almost seemed that nightfall was earlier than usual.

Peering from the window into the half-light, Jamie thought that Porthcurno looked a lonely cove. Jamie said, 'You know, during storms or at night this is just the place which might well be haunted by ghosts, ghouls or goblins, or even Old Nick himself.'

Anthony laughed to hear a favourite line from his own storytelling quoted back to him. He knew the stories would be safe for another generation. And though it was a rough evening, the inn was warm and the company good. Jamie was worried though. They had made nothing in Penzance and could not afford a room at the inn. Where would they sleep on such a rough night?

Then, late in the evening, a stranger in the inn leapt to his feet. Looking at his pocket watch he exclaimed it was nearly midnight. What would he do? He'd missed the last coach, or jingle as they were called then. 'That's alright,' said a swarthy sailor in the corner of the bar. 'I have to get to Penzance tonight; you can sail with me. You can easily recognise my ship: a black hull, just the one mast, square rigged, with a tender moored astern.'

But when, a few minutes later, the sailor left the bar, the landlord spoke to the stranger, 'Best you don't sail with him, take a room here for the night'.

'No,' said the stranger, 'I have to get to Penzance.'

'Not with him you don't', said the landlord, who seized the stranger and led him to the window. Together they looked out at the cove.

'The ship's gone!' cried the stranger.

'Aha,' said Anthony, 'you only just missed it. I saw it myself!'

Jamie was about to say something when Anthony kicked him under the table and continued mysteriously. 'Yes I saw the Black Ship. You know, it didn't head out to sea. It just turned, sailed straight through the breakers on the shore, over the sands and up the valley. There was no crew to be seen, but it sailed as surely over the dry land as if it had been on water. On it went across the land until eventually it vanished like smoke.'

'They say that to see the Black Ship is bad luck,' said Anthony James, 'but to sail with it is to share its fate. The story is from before your time and before mine, but not that long ago.'

Then the droll teller continued to tell his story:

The Black Ship belongs to a strange man who came from the sea and went to live up at Chygwidden. No one knew where he originally came from. He had a servant, a stern-looking foreign man who never spoke to anyone but his master. No one knew what they did for a living. Some said they were privateers or smugglers.

They kept their boat down at Porthcurno and at first light they would set sail, never returning until dark. Often they would stay out all night, especially if the weather was wild.

When not at sea they were out hunting. Day or night, especially if a storm was raging, there was this strange man, accompanied either by his servant or by the Devil, and the midnight howling of his dogs disturbed all the country for miles round.

Eventually this mysterious chap died, and his servant asked some locals to help carry his coffin to St Levan churchyard, which they did. The corpse was laid in the grave. The dogs and the servant stood beside. But then as soon as the earth was thrown on the coffin, both servant and dogs vanished. At exactly the same moment the boat disappeared from the cove. A great storm choked Porthcurno with sand, and from that day to this no mortal has been able to keep a boat there. If you see the Black Ship you should shun it, for it's an omen of bad luck.

Anthony concluded, triumphantly, 'So that my friend, is why you should take a room here tonight!'

'All right then,' said the stranger, 'I will take a room for the night please landlord. But droll teller, you've told me that seeing the Black Ship of Porthcurno brings bad luck. Do you know something to bring me some good luck to counteract it?'

'Yes, I can help you there,' said Anthony James. 'but the first thing is to cross the storyteller's palm with silver, for saving you from an awful fate.'

The stranger produced his purse and quizzically pressed some coins into Anthony's outstretched hand.

'Why thank you, sir,' said Anthony, pretending to be surprised. 'Now I remember when I was in Summercourt. Everyone gathered to watch a maid throw a pig's nose over her house for good luck. "Bound to work" they said. The pig had been slaughtered the day before and she got its nose. Curiously the ears were somehow still attached. She turned her back to the house, seized the pig's ears and threw the nose up over her head.'

'Did it work? asked the incredulous stranger.

'Oh yes,' said Anthony, 'it flew clean over the house.'

'Yes, but did it bring her good luck?'

'I dunno, but at that moment the parson was coming down the lane on his new-fangled velocipede. As befits a man of the cloth, his mind was on higher things. But the parson didn't expect that the higher things would include a pig's nose flying down from heaven, and it knocked him clean off his velocipede and into the pond. He never had the same view of religion again.'

The room erupted into laughter. Then the landlord showed the stranger to his room.

Jamie looked at the rain that was now falling outside. 'What about us?' he asked.

'Don't worry', said Anthony.

Just then the landlord reappeared. He was chuckling to himself.

'Thank you friend,' he said to Anthony, 'that was neatly done. I'll give old Billy his tot tomorrow for looking dark and suspicious as usual. But I dare say you and your boy would like the spare room?'

11

Uðnek

St Levan

After Porthcurno the track climbed steeply, but soon curved inland to the hamlet of St Levan. Jamie could see the tower of the church up the valley.

'So who was St Levan?' asked the inquisitive boy.

'Yet another old Celtic saint,' replied Anthony.

Then a voice behind them boomed out, 'There are more saints in Cornwall than there are in heaven!' It was the curate who had joined them. 'But this one was a powerful man,' he continued, 'Selevan was his proper name. Come with me to the churchyard and I'll show you something.' As they walked towards the church, the curate said this:

SELEVAN

Selevan was a good man. He had a chapel on the cliff edge; the bay below is still called Porth Chapel. Down the cliff he had a holy well; its water is used for baptisms to this very day. In the churchyard of St Levan is a great circular stone with a split down the middle. It was used as a seat by Selevan himself. He liked to sit here when he was tired after doing his fishing. But apparently the people then were not as righteous as they should have been. So, like the Old Testament prophets, he struck the stone with his staff and the stone split in two. Then he prayed over the stone. He addressed his flock and prophesied that when a mounted and loaded pack horse could be ridden through the split in the rock, then the world would come to an end.

When with panniers astride,
A Pack Horse can ride,
Through St Levan's Stone,
The world will be done.

I think Selevan meant that the size of the gap between the two halves is dependent on the sinfulness of congregation! No one yet has tried to ride through it; it looks far too narrow. But of late it does seem that the gap between the stones is getting a bit wider. So you never know!

Then the curate's wife appeared and they chatted about times past. Jamie was amazed at Anthony's ability to be relaxed with almost anyone he met. 'Perhaps,' he thought, 'as Anthony can't see them he doesn't jump to conclusions. He assumes the best of everybody unless they prove otherwise.'

'Friends,' said the curate, 'the old law of hospitality is not dead in Cornwall. Come to my cottage for supper this evening. You can sing, play and tell tales for your supper, and then if you wish you can sleep in the stable.'

That supper was a fine meal, and welcome too. Afterwards, by the fire, Anthony explained that perhaps he ought to tell a local tale. He said, 'This is a fine old story. My father once heard it told in Cornish by old Mr Boson in Newlyn. He called it "Jowan Chy an Horth"; "John of the House of the Ram". But now it's popular in English too and it's called "Tom of Chyannor", "Tom the Tinner", or even the "Three Points of Wisdom".'

TOM THE TINNER

Tom Tresidder the tinner lived at Chy an Horth, the House of the Ram, near St Levan. Now Tom was a tin streamer, for in those days you still could sluice the black tin sand from the streambeds. But eventually all the tin had gone. Tom and his family fell on hard times. Tom had his wife to support and his daughter; sixteen years old she was, and the very image of her mother. So reluctantly Tom said a fond farewell to them both and set out to find work.

He had heard there was work to be had over in the east. So he walked for a day and he walked for another day, and close to sunset he reached a farm near Praze an Beeble. There the farmer and his wife were kindly people, so Tom asked to be taken on as a farmhand. He agreed to work for a year for two gold pieces. For a year he worked hard and he worked well. After twelve months the farmer said to him, 'Here is your pay, but it's been a hard year. If you give it back to me I will give you something worth more than silver and gold.' Tom thought, 'If it's worth more than silver and gold I'd best be having it.' So Tom agreed, but what the farmer gave him was a piece of advice; 'a point of wisdom' he called it, and the advice he got was this: 'Never lodge in a house where an old man is married to a young wife.'

Then Tom thought, 'I still have nothing to take back to my wife and daughter.' So he agreed to work for another year for two more gold pieces. For another year he worked hard and he worked well. After twelve months the farmer said, 'Here is your pay, but it's been a hard year. If you give it back I will give you something worth more than strength.' Tom thought, 'If it really is worth more than strength then I'd best be having it.' So Tom again agreed, but again what the farmer gave him was a 'point of wisdom', and the advice he got was this: 'Never forsake the old road for the new.'

Then Tom thought, 'I still have nothing to take back to my wife and daughter.' So he agreed to work for yet another year for two more gold pieces. For that year he worked hard and he worked well. After twelve months the farmer said, 'Here is your pay, but it's been a hard year. If you give it back I will give you something worth more than gold and silver and strength.' So once again Tom agreed, but once again what the farmer gave him was a piece of advice. The farmer said it was the best 'point of wisdom' of all, and the advice he gave to Tom was this: 'Never swear to anything seen through glass.'

Then Tom decided that although he had nothing to show for three years work he would return to his wife and daughter. The farmer's wife gave him a fine slab of heavy cake to take with him.

On the road, Tom soon met some fellow travellers. They were merchants and they drove pack horses laden with wool from Helston Fair. They were going to Treen, not far from where Tom lived, so he was delighted to have some company on the road.

That night they reached an inn. As the door was opened, Tom saw the landlord was an old man, but the landlady was a young woman. He remembered the first advice, 'Never lodge in a house where an old man is married to a young wife.' So he asked to sleep in the stable. That night as he lay there he heard voices. Looking through a knothole he saw the young landlady talking to a monk, discussing how they had murdered the old landlord. But the monk stood close to the knothole and Tom was able to secretly cut a fragment of fabric from the monk's gown with his penknife.

Next day Tom woke to find a gallows outside, for his friends the merchants had already been found guilty of the landlord's murder. But Tom produced the fragment of cloth and told what he had heard, so the merchants were set free and again they set off on the road, with many promises of rewards for Tom when their trading was over.

After a while they came to a fork in the road where a new shortcut had been made. 'Come with us on the new road', said the merchants, but Tom remembered the second piece of advice, 'Never forsake the old road for the new.' So alone he took the old road. He'd only gone a few yards when he heard a hue and cry from over the hill. He ran across and found his new friends were being attacked by robbers. 'One and all!' cried Tom as he struck out with his walking stick and soon they sent the robbers flying. Then the merchants continued in safety with many thanks and more promises of reward.

So after two days walking Tom got home. Looking in the window, he thought he saw his wife kissing a young man. His grip tightened on his stick and he was about to burst in when he remembered the third advice, 'Never swear to anything seen through glass.' So he put his stick back in his belt and he gently went inside to find it was his daughter, now a young woman and still the very image of her mother, saying goodnight to her fiancée, Jan the cobbler.

Of course they were all delighted at being together again. But then Tom had to explain to his wife that for three years work he had earned only cake and wisdom, to which his wife replied it seemed that he had earned nothing but cake. She was so vexed that she picked up the cake and threw it at Tom with all her might. Tom ducked and the flying cake missed him and smashed against the wall. As it did so it broke into pieces. Out fell not two or four or six, but fifteen gold pieces, all wrapped in a piece of paper. On the paper was written, 'The reward of an honest man'.

12

Dewdhek

PORTHGWARRA

As the sun climbed higher they continued to the west. The sun was warm on their backs and long shadows stretched ahead of them. On their left the sea was bright, the cliffs shone gold in the sunlight. Again the path climbed steeply out of the valley, and after a short distance curved into yet another inlet.

There Jamie was fascinated by the manmade caves, with winches to pull small boats up the beach and even a tunnel carved through the rock.

'Was the tunnel for smugglers?' asked Jamie.

'I'm afraid not,' said Anthony, 'people here used to harvest the seaweed from the beach to use as fertilizer on the land. But the steep rocks at the head of the inlet meant they had to carry the seaweed on a pack horse or in a little hand cart. So they got miners from St Just to come and make this tunnel so they could take a decent horse and cart right down to the water's edge.'

Then suddenly heard a sound. It was a sigh, as if from someone in despair, but it seemed to come from the sea. 'Don't worry lad,' said Anthony, 'it's a natural hydrophone. There's a rock out there called the Runnel Stone. It has a hole in it, and as the swell forces air through the hole it makes that very human sound.'

Jamie said, 'It's as if someone is very sad. Sometimes mother sounds like that.'

'This is Porthgwarra', announced Anthony. 'They call it the Lovers' Cove. They say there is a sad ghost here, perhaps two.' Anthony drew a deep breath, and then he told this story:

THE LOVERS OF PORTHGWARRA

Once there were two young lovers called Nancy and William, but I'm afraid their love did not run smooth. Nancy's parents disapproved of the young man. Her father was a rich farmer, but her lover was only his servant, the son of a fisherman, and they reckoned William was not good enough for their daughter. They tried telling Nancy to have nothing to do with him, but of course she took no notice at all. So they had the young man fired from his job, and they ensured that no one else round about would give him a job either. Eventually William was forced to emigrate to get work.

The day before the young man was to due set sail, the lovers met here in this cove of Porthgwarra. Here they kissed, said their goodbyes and by the light of the full moon they vowed that living or dead they would meet again after three years, and with that they tearfully parted.

It was just about three years later, and on one evening one of the old ladies of the village was sat up on the cliff top above Porthgwarra. There was a full moon, and she was enjoying the beauty of the moonlight reflecting on the tranquil sea. Then, by that moonlight, she saw a pretty girl go down into the cove and sit on a rock, with the waves rippling at her feet.

But the old woman could see that the tide was coming in. Nonetheless the girl just sat on the rock looking out to sea until she was nearly surrounded by the rising tide. The old woman called out a warning, but the girl seemed not to hear. She just sat there with the tide coming in around her.

The old woman knew that something would have to be done. She decided to go down into the cove and warn the girl of the danger. But while she was going down the cliff path, for a moment she lost sight of the girl. When the old woman next saw the rock, she could see that the young maid had a handsome sailor by her side, with his arm around her waist.

The old woman thought that help had arrived, and her warning was no longer required. So she sat down again, watching the moonlight on the water, and occasionally glancing at couple on the rock. But then she saw that they just sat on the rock as the tide rose and washed around them. 'They must be mad' thought the old woman and she called out a warning. Suddenly, as the water grew higher and higher, together they seemed to float off into the water. The old woman thought she heard their voices; but they were not frightened. Instead there was quiet music, like the voice of doves, singing together in the moonlight.

Down, down into the sea floated the lovers. As the old woman watched they looked straight at her. Then, smiling like angels and embracing, they sank into the depths and were lost from sight.

They say that the body of the young woman was found a day or two later in a cove nearby. Some days after that, news reached Cornwall that the young man had been lost at sea, the very night that the old lady had seen the couple on the rock, the very night the young woman had drowned.

But you can still see them there, when the night is still and the moon shines on the tranquil sea. Sometimes you can still hear the young girl sighing for her lost lover, and local people will still remind you that to them, Porthgwarra is always the 'Lovers' Cove'.

Jamie looked at Anthony and saw there were tears in the man's eyes. 'What is it? Are you alright?'

'Yes,' said Anthony, 'I'm alright. But that is a story very near to my heart. There's a lot of it that is rather close to home.'

At that moment their attention was drawn by a black bird that flew low across the cliff top. Its flight was a series of short, low swoops and its call was persistent.

On hearing it, Anthony said, 'Good afternoon, Sire' and doffed his cap. 'Do you know who that is?' he asked, and Jamie shook his head.

King Arthur as a Chough

That black bird is called a chough, and it's the royal bird of Cornwall. You find it on old coats of arms. You can recognize it because its beak and legs and feet are red. But that bird is none other than Arthur, the great King of Old Britain.

After his last battle Arthur was never seen again in human form. But he never died; he turned into a chough instead. To this day he's still here, keeping an eye on Cornwall. If he's ever needed then he will again adopt his human form and return to rescue his countrymen. So when anyone sees him they should greet him in a manner befitting a King. When you see a chough, doff your cap. Say to him, 'Good afternoon, Sire.' After all, he is the once and future King.

'Perhaps that's a lesson for us,' said Jamie. Anthony looked thoughtful; then he said, 'Come on boy. We have to pass Land's End and reach Sennen before nightfall.'

13

Tardhek

SENNEN

At Land's End Anthony James and Jamie paused. 'Can you see the lighthouse?' asked Anthony.

'I can see a tower', replied Jamie.

'When I left Cornwall there was talk of building such a thing. Now they've done it, not that I'll ever see it. I understand it's called the Longships Light. It'll certainly help sailors in these parts, but there are a few landsmen that will be less happy. They may not deliberately cause ships to wreck, but they are happy to profit if they do.'

As the coast swung to the north, Jamie could see a striking headland. 'That will be Pedn-Men-Du', said Anthony when Jamie described the scene. '"Pedn" or "penn" means head, or headland; "Men" means rock and "Du" means black. So it means Black Rock Head. Just this side of it you may be able to see the Irish Lady.' Anthony grinned.

'I can't see any ladies,' said Jamie, 'but just off shore there is a curiously shaped rock.'

'That's her', said Anthony.

The Irish Lady

Long ago a ship from Ireland was wrecked at night on this very rock. Everyone on board was drowned apart from one lady. The morning after the wreck she was seen sitting on the top of the rock. But the storm was still raging, and it was quite impossible to rescue her. The seas were too rough and the cliffs too steep. Days and nights passed as the people watched the poor woman from the shore, but they still could not reach her. Eventually the poor lady died and her body was washed into the sea.

But since that day, when the winds and waves are high, fishermen often see a lady peacefully sitting on this rock with a rose in her mouth, quite indifferent to the raging of the storm.

Shortly after Land's End the rocky coast opened out in a magnificent sandy bay. Long lines of breakers marched in from the Atlantic and crashed on the silver sand. 'Whitesand Bay,' announced Anthony, 'I'd know that sound anywhere. The sand here is the cleanest and whitest in all the world, and the village is called Sennen.'

They made their way past a small quay and cottages sheltering on the steep hillside until they came to an inn. 'This'll do for us, lad. The Old Success has been welcoming storytellers since the time of Charles II.'

The inn was a jigsaw of dark timbers. A good fire burned in the grate. Leaning on the bar was a grizzled, weather-beaten character wearing a harum-scarum overcoat. From one pocket protruded what appeared to be a homemade post horn, battered but gleaming. Bits of twig stuck out of the other pocket. Jamie guided Anthony to the bar. There, Anthony turned to the coated figure.

'No pilchards today then', he said. Jamie marvelled how Anthony, though blind, seemed to perceive so much about him.

'Not for a week or two yet,' came the reply, 'then we'll hear the old "towl roos" again.'

'Towl roos?' asked Jamie.

'I'm the Sennen Huer and that's my cry', said the coated figure. 'It means "shoot the net". I used to fish till I broke my leg.

Now I peg it up the hill out the back with my old telescope. When I see a shoal disturbing the water then I blow my horn to alert the other seine lads. Look there.' The huer indicated out of the window. Pulled up on the beach were numbers of small craft, but three, larger than most, were loaded with nets and gear. By way of demonstration the huer pulled the horn from his pocket and the assembled company put their fingers in their ears as a series of painful notes ricocheted around the low-ceilinged room.

'I shout "Hevva, hevva, hevva!" and the lads row out. I have a fuzzy bush in each hand to tell 'em which way to go. When they're near the shoal I shout "Towl roos!" and they shoot the seine. Then the seine boats take the net right round the shoal. They close off the seine with a tuck-net, then they row the shoal ashore. There they tuck the pilchards into baskets, ready for the jousters, fish sellers that is, to take over to Penzance.'

Jamie was rather overwhelmed by the onslaught of new words, but felt he understood enough to nod his head and say, 'I see!' Anthony turned away.

The huer continued reflectively, 'The rest of the time we just have to catch what we can, but it's not easy. Here, boy,' he said to Jamie confidentially, 'did you ever hear of the Hooper of Sennen?'

'No sir,' said Jamie, and then the story began:

THE HOOPER OF SENNEN

The Hooper of Sennen is a great bank of mist. It stretches from Aire Point to Pedn-Men-Du. The mist is so thick you can't see through it. Some people say that the mist is itself an evil spirit. When the Hooper is down, then it's best not to put to sea. A great storm is sure to follow, or even worse.

There once was an old fisherman who used to laugh at such tales. In fact he used to laugh at most things and if you asked him the time of day, he would charge you for it! And they say he never went to chapel!

Well one day the Hooper was down, and most of the local fisherman took to mending their nets and such like. But that old scoffer, he said it was all nothing but superstition. After all, although the Hooper was on the sea, the sun was still shining on the sands and the waves were tiny. The other fisherman warned them, but of course he and his son took no notice and set out in their boat. The son stood in the bow with a pitchfork, and the old man at the stern had a threshing flail. They sailed into the Hooper, with the young fellow stabbing into the mist with the pitchfork and the old man beating the fog with the threshel. On shore, the listeners could hear them shouting abuse at the sea and cursing the Hooper. But the voices got fainter and fainter, and then suddenly stopped.

Do you know, they were never seen again. A great cloud swept in; it made the day as dark as night. Then the waves and wind rose up and beat on Sennen for three days. When the storm abated the wreckage was there on the shore. When they found the old man the pitchfork was in his chest. When they found the boy he had the flail wrapped round his neck. The biggest piece of the wreckage was the transom plank, and that had great teeth marks in it.

Now the Hooper isn't seen so often these days. It's as if somehow it, or what it conceals, has been satisfied. But when the Hooper is down it is best to stay ashore.

14

Peswardhek

St Just

After Sennen they soon arrived at St Just. In those days it was a very small town, huddled around the market square by the church, but still with a coaching inn at which tales could be told. There they met John Davey, the schoolmaster who was a great fiddle player. Billy Foss, the mason, came in with his oboe and both men swapped yarns with Anthony. Their ready wit and the bright tunes of the instruments soon attracted a crowd. Then, as the embers settled, Anthony held court.

Jamie sat with a glass of small beer in his hand. In those days it was what almost everyone drank, unless you lived by a spring or well. As he listened to the story he was reminded that many lads of his age had to work in the tin mines. Even young girls worked as 'bal maidens' on the surface, crushing rocks or pushing trams. Jamie had never been below ground and he shuddered at the thought. But he laughed at the story, and like everyone else he joined in the chorus.

THE WRESTLERS OF CARN KENIDJACK

Now Jackie and Jan were two poor mining lads. They were so poor they didn't even have a belt between them to hold up their trousers. Instead their trousers were tied up with hairy string left over from baling the hay. Now on a Friday, like any other working men, they looked forward to an evening in the kiddleywink. But the lads lived in St Just, and in those days the people of St Just were so upright and virtuous that, unlike today, there was not a single pub in the town. You can see how things have changed! But back then, to wet your whistle you had to walk all the way from St Just to Morvah, four miles away.

One Friday evening Jackie and Jan were about to leave when their mother called them. 'Do you know what night it is?' she asked. They shook their heads. She said, 'Tonight is Hallowe'en. After the witching hour you may see ghosts, ghouls, goblins and even Old Nick himself. So you must be home by midnight.'

The lads promised and set off to Morvah. Down the hill and across the stream at Nancherrow, then up past Botallack and Pendeen, apprehensively skirting the slopes of Carn Kenidjack. For on a dark night it is said that there you can see flickering lights and hear strange hooting sounds – surely the work of ghosts, ghouls, goblins and even Old Nick himself.

Eventually they reached Morvah and soon in the kiddleywink they were cracking jokes, playing tunes, singing songs and swapping stories. And because it was Hallowe'en the jokes, the tunes, the songs and stories were all about ghosts, ghouls, goblins and even Old Nick himself. It was so much fun that Jackie and Jan completely failed to notice the passing of time. Then suddenly there was the clock on the wall chiming midnight, and the lads knew they were in the most terrible trouble.

They put down their glasses, rushed outside and started running down the road. They hoped that if they were only a little bit late, they would only be in a little bit of trouble. Then, as they ran down the road, they thought perhaps they could save even more time and be in even less trouble if they cut across the common just below Carn Kenidjack. So it was that five minutes after midnight on Hallowe'en, Jackie and Jan stepped off the road. They hadn't been off the road for more than five minutes when they heard the sound of a horse being galloped through the night. They had to throw themselves off the path to avoid being ridden down.

Jackie called out to the rider, 'Hey, that's no way to ride at night.'

The horse stopped and turned. The rider wore a cloak with hood, but they could see his eyes glowing as red as coals in the darkness. He said, 'I'm going up to Carn Kenidjack to watch the wrestling. Why don't you come too?' Now there's no sport a Cornish lad likes more than wrestling, and suddenly it seemed the most natural thing in the world to follow the commanding stranger up the hill. Now don't any of you ever do anything as foolish as that!

Up and up the lads climbed. To their surprise, at the top of the carn they found a grassy bank surrounding a 'plen an gwari', a 'playing place' used for events like wrestling. In the middle of this ring were two huge wrestlers, and seated all around were ghosts, ghouls, goblins and even Old Nick himself, with his eyes still blazing red.

Then the wrestling began. It was like no match you or I have ever seen. The wrestlers were ten feet tall. With every fall you could hear the crunch of breaking bones, the ripping of sinews and the tearing of flesh. It was just like Penzance on a Friday night! Every brutal fall was applauded by the ghosts, ghouls, goblins and even Old Nick himself.

Eventually one of the wrestlers managed to lift the other high into the air and smashed his opponent down onto a granite rock. The poor, defeated wrestler gave a groan and then was silent. Then all the ghosts carried the victor round to where Old Nick was sitting and they all gathered around the throne to see the winner get his prize. But the poor loser just lay there, motionless on the ground.

'I reckon we ought to help him', said Jackie.

'Darn right', said Jan.

So Jackie and Jan scrambled into the ring to where the poor giant lay.

'Is he alive?' asked Jackie.

'Only just', said Jan.

'I reckon we should get a doctor', said Jackie.

'I think he's took far gone for that', said Jan.

'In that case I reckon we should get a priest!' said Jackie.

'I don't think we got time for that', said Jan.

'Well darn it, do 'ee know any prayers?' said Jackie. Now I'm sorry to tell you that Jackie and Jan did not pay much attention in chapel, but…

'I think know one', said Jan.

'Well you better say it now', said Jackie.

So Jan started, 'Our Father, which art in heaven, hallowed be thy name. Thy will be done…'

And at that instant he stopped. On the back of his neck all the hairs were standing on end; the feeling you get when you know someone is watching you. The lads looked up and there, right behind them were all the ghosts, ghouls, goblins and even Old Nick himself, his eyes blazing red.

They saw Old Nick raise his arm, they saw him point his crooked finger straight at them, they saw his chest heave to draw breath and they saw him open his mouth to speak. But do you know, they didn't wait to hear what he was going to say! The lads ran as fast as their legs could carry them down towards St Just. Behind them came all the ghosts, ghouls, goblins, and even old Nick himself. And every yard they ran, the ghosts, ghouls, goblins and even Old Nick himself got closer.

Now Jackie and Jan remembered that ghosts dare not cross running water. If they could only get across the stream at Nancherrow they would be safe. But Jackie had got the stitch, and with every pace the ghosts, ghouls, goblins, and even Old Nick himself got closer and closer.

And now Jan's laces were coming undone! Every second the ghosts, ghouls, goblins and even Old Nick himself got closer and closer and closer.

And they were just one pace from the bridge when the biggest, ugliest, fiercest, hungriest goblin reached out and seized them both by the seat of the pants. With a snarl of triumph he opened his jaws to reveal the sharpest teeth you can imagine. He was just about to bite their heads off. You'd have thought they would have been gobbled up in an instant.

But Jackie and Jan were just poor mining lads. Their trousers were only held up with old hairy string. The string broke with a mighty twang, and so it was that Jackie and Jan crossed the bridge, but their trousers never did!

Now that's the tale the lads told their mother to explain how they arrived home from the pub at one o'clock in the morning with no trousers on. They told her, she told me and I told you. That probably makes it almost true!

15

ZENNOR

Leaving St Just, Anthony and Jamie followed the route of Jackie and Jan. They walked down the steep hill and crossed the stream at Nancherrow. When Jamie pointed out a distinctive milestone, Anthony remarked that it had probably been carved by Billy Foss. Then the way led up past Botallack and Pendeen, skirting the slopes of Carn Kenidjack. Jamie secretly looked up to try and see any ghosts, ghouls, goblins or even Old Nick himself, but the gentle gorse-covered hillside was peaceful and benign.

As they passed Morvah, Anthony remarked that on the first Sunday in August people came from miles around to Morvah Fair. 'There are animals and sports and games, and drinking too', he grinned. 'There's an old saying, "three on a horse to Morvah Fair" and they say that a quarter of an acre wouldn't hold all the horses ridden to the fair. That's a lot for this part of the world. Morvah is famous for other things too', he continued, laughing.

THE BELL-RINGER OF MORVAH

One dark night, the citizens of the parish of Morvah were sleeping soundly in their beds. Suddenly, on the stroke of midnight, the mournful sound of the church bell echoed across the fields. A single bell was steadily tolling as if announcing a death or summoning all to a funeral. The sexton, parson, clerk and parishioners too were woken by this untimely sound and they all rushed to the scene to confront its monstrous cause. The parson had his bell, book and candle and was saying special prayers to ward off evil. They thought it might be some evil spirit or even Old Nick himself.

When they reached the church they found the door was open. Strange sounds came from the dark interior. By flickering candlelight they carefully crept inside. There they found a hungry cow, contentedly chewing on the bell rope! For a while they went round bragging that Morvah has the holiest cows! But now times are so hard they say there isn't enough grass in the parish of Morvah to feed a hungry short-horn.

They followed the winding track until late in the day they reached the village of Zennor. There they were greeted by the local people, and that evening they all gathered in Chy Pons (Bridge House). There the miller held court; he was a merry man. 'Right then,' he said, 'it's time I told you a story.'

THE MERMAID OF ZENNOR

Between Land's End and Scilly is the lost land of Lyonesse, drowned by the great storm of 11 November 1099. The old folks used to say that when such a storm is about to happen again, you can hear the last bell of Lyonesse ringing out a warning.

In the village of Zennor there once lived a fisherman called Mathy Trewhella. He was a fine lad. Every Sunday he sang in the choir and he rang the bell at church; they only had one bell in those days. His steady tolling would summon everyone to church. Then he sang so well that more people listened to him than to the rector. He sang so well people came miles

to hear him. It was said that his singing was so beautiful it could entrance a mermaid. But the old women of the village always said, 'Mark my words, no good will come of it!'

One day a young lady joined the congregation. She had green eyes and long golden hair. She wore a long silver cloak that nearly touched the ground. She sat on her own at the back of the church and spoke to no one else. But she listened most intently whenever Mathy sang. Soon rumours spread that Mathy had been seen walking out with this charming young lady and everyone was very pleased for them both. They made a handsome couple, and people were glad they had found each other and were happy. All but the old women of the village; they just said, 'Mark my words, no good will come of it!'

Then one Sunday the parishioners were late for church. No one had come to ring the bell. People thought that perhaps Mathy had overslept, or perhaps been out late courting his young lady. Mostly they smiled and didn't mind. All but the old women of the village; they just said, 'Mark my words, no good will come of it!'

But as the hours and then days passed, it seemed that Mathy had completely disappeared. Never again did he ring the bell in church or sing in the choir. He and the golden-haired girl were never seen again. People wondered if they had eloped together and wished them well. All except the old women of the village – and you know what they said!

Now, many weeks later, people were surprised to hear a bell ringing. But it was not the church bell. It had the deepest sound they had ever heard and it seemed to come from beneath the sea. The steady tolling of the bell seemed familiar to all who heard it. But then some old folk who remembered the ancient legends said it must be the last bell of Lyonesse being rung under the ocean to warn of a great storm. So the people of Zennor pulled the boats up the beach, shuttered the windows and barred the doors. They drove the sheep and cattle to high ground inland. The old women of the village nearly smiled as they repeated, 'We told you, no good would come of it!'

Then the greatest storm that Zennor had ever known arrived. For one, two, three days the storm raged, but the precautions they had taken kept them all safe. No one was hurt and no livestock were lost.

But then as the storm died, when people were unbolting the doors and pulling back the shutters, a wide-eyed sea captain rode into town. 'News,' he cried, 'I bring strange news for the people of Zennor.'

The people gathered round and the sea captain started to speak. 'I anchored my ship in St Ives Bay to shelter from the storm. But as the waves abated I heard someone calling. I looked over the rail and there was a mermaid with golden hair and green eyes. 'Move your ship, captain,' she said, 'your anchor is blocking my door, and soon my husband Mathy will return from his task of tolling his great bell. He will want to come in to his wife and children.'

'Is that Mathy Trewhella you are speaking of?' asked the captain.

'Yes,' said the mermaid, 'it is he, and now he lives with me under the sea. But whenever a storm is due he will toll a warning to his friends in Zennor on the last bell of Lyonesse.'

That is how the people of Zennor learned the fate of Mathy Trewhella. In her honour, a picture of the mermaid was carved on one of the pews in Zennor Church. It is still there, to this very day. And the people of Zennor sleep sound. They know that if ever there is another great storm then Mathy Trewhella will ring the last bell of Lyonesse to sound a warning to his friends in Zennor. All except the old women of the village; they still say, 'Mark my words, no good will come of it!'

There was applause and laughter. It seemed that the fun might come to an end. But then the door burst open. Jamie was amazed to see a group of men dressed in outlandish clothing. One man wore a woman's dress! All had masks made of strips of cloth. One played a fife, another had a fiddle. They sang songs, told outlandish tales and ended by step dancing on the stone flags of the mill. Then, as suddenly as they had arrived, they were gone. 'Off to the rectory,' someone said, 'they'll get a good supper there.'

Anthony sensed that Jamie's mind was full of questions. 'Guisers', he said. 'They are just men in disguise, so no one knows who they are. Sometimes they put soot on their faces or wear masks, whatever is handy really. They disguise themselves so the high and mighty won't know who's causing mayhem, but it's only harmless fun. The people hereabouts are very close.'

GRANDFATHER AND THE STILE

Once there was a poor family in Zennor struggling to make ends meet. There was a tinner and his wife, and his old father too. They all lived in a tiny two-roomed cottage. Then one day the young wife announced that she was expecting a baby. Initially they were full of joy. But as the weeks passed the couple grew more and more gloomy. The cottage was tiny. When the baby arrived there would not be room for its grandfather. What was to be done? He was too old and frail to live on his own. The couple talked long into the night trying to decide what to do. Then one morning the young tinner took his dad's arm. 'I'm sorry father,' he said, 'but when the baby comes there won't be room for you here. So I'm afraid it's the workhouse for you.'

The tinner steered the old man outside and started to lead him up the hill towards the 'Eagles Nest'; it was the workhouse in those days. It was a steep climb and after a while they rested at a style in the dry-stone wall. As they rested they looked down at the village of Zennor, and the little cottage and the fields about it. 'You know,' said the old man, 'this is the very style at which I rested when I took my father up to the workhouse.' The tinner looked at his father, and tears filled the young man's eyes. Then the two of them walked back down the hill.

'I'll remember that', said Jamie.

16

St Ives

Walking north-east on the rugged track, Anthony James explained they were heading for St Ives. Chuckling to himself, he recited this rhyme:

> As I was going to St Ives
> I met a man with seven wives
> Each wife had seven sacks
> Each sack had seven cats
> Each cat had seven kits
> Kits, cats, sacks, wives
> How many were going to St Ives?

After a pause he asked, 'Well then, how many?'

'I don't know,' said Jamie, 'dozens?'

'Try again!'

'Hundreds?'

'Try again!'

'Thousands?'

'No,' said Anthony, 'the answer is one.'

'How can that be?' asked Jamie. Then he looked at Anthony's broad grin.

'It's a trick!' said the boy.

Trying not to laugh, Anthony explained the riddle to the boy. 'If the poet met that man with seven wives, then they must have been going the other way, or at least standing still. So the only person actually going to St Ives was the man who invented the riddle.'

Jamie looked very unconvinced!

JOHN KNILL

Above the town they found a crowd gathering near a three-sided granite obelisk, some fifty feet high.

Anthony announced, 'That's John Knill's Steeple; built by an old mayor of St Ives. If people are starting to gather we must not waste time.' They hurried down into the town, to the Guildhall. There they were greeted by the clerk. 'That's William Allen,' said Anthony, 'self-educated, but a good man. He plays the fiddle and knows dozens of songs!'

At half past ten some grandly dressed men came outside. A small iron chest with three locks was placed in front of them. The Mayor of St Ives took a key and undid the first lock, the town customs officer undid the second, and the vicar unlocked the third. The Mayor took out a scroll. To the assembled company he read that Mr Knill had directed that every five years, on the feast day of St James, the following money should be spent:

> £10 on a dinner at the George and Dragon Inn for the Trustees (the Mayor, Vicar and Customs Officer), and two guests each.
>
> £5 for ten little girls, the daughters of fishermen, tinners or seamen. In return the girls shall, between ten and twelve o'clock, dance for a quarter of an hour at least, on the ground near the Steeple, and after the dance sing the 100th psalm 'to the fine old tune' as sung in St Ives church.
>
> £1 for a fiddler to play for the girls while dancing and singing, and also to play before them on their return to St Ives.
>
> £2 to two widows.
>
> £1 for white ribbon for breast knots for the dancers.

£1 for a vellum book for the Clerk to the Trustees to enter a Minute of the proceedings.

£5 to the man and wife, widower or widow who shall raise the greatest family of legitimate children who have reached the age of ten years.

At the last announcement there was a wry cheer from the crowd and much laughter. Then, the speech over, they formed a procession. In the lead were the Mayor, customs officer and vicar. Then came the Mayor's mace-bearer and a master of ceremonies with a top hat and a baton. Then marched Jamie, Anthony merrily playing his fiddle, the two widows, and then ten little girls dressed in white with flowers in their hair. A crowd followed, some couples dancing to the music.

It was a steep climb to the steeple, but they were there before noon. Anthony played the fiddle as the girls joined hands and danced around the steeple three times. As they danced they sang, 'Shun the banter of the bay, Hasten upward, come away…' Many onlookers joined in and even the widows found someone to dance with! After fifteen minutes everyone sang the 100th Psalm, 'All people that on earth do dwell'. Then the vicar gave a blessing, and they all walked down to the town.

The George and Dragon was on the west side of the marketplace, facing the church. It was a grand building and unlike most inns they visited, its patrons were very well-to-do. Jamie felt out of place but Anthony, of course, saw none of this and relaxed at a table, spinning yarns with whoever gave him the time of day. But then William Allen came in with his fiddle and with Anthony struck up a merry tune. Jamie felt much more relaxed.

In a lull in the merrymaking, Jamie piped up, 'Who was St Ive? I never heard of such a saint.'

ST IVE

Legends say that the area near St Ives Bay was settled by Irish immigrants in about the fourth century. That was before anyone was Christian there or here. But then St Patrick converted the Irish. Ive, or Ia as the churchmen called her, was an Irish princess, and she was converted to Christianity when she was very young. But those were very warlike times, and Ive resolved to spread the new Christian message of peace and love. Perhaps she thought that the Cornish particularly needed this message!

Then Ive found that a holy man and woman, Fingar and Piala, were going on an expedition to bring Christianity to Cornwall. She went to join them, but when she reached the harbour she found they had left without her. The sail could be seen far away on the horizon. She was very disappointed and sat down on the sand to pray. A clover leaf floating on the water caught her eye, and she tried to push it under the water with her staff, just to make it sink. But the leaf did not sink. Not only did it float, but it grew bigger and bigger till it was the size of a small boat. Ive climbed on board and soon a fair wind carried her straight to Cornwall. Her journey was so speedy she got here before her companions who had set off earlier. The place she landed has been called St Ives ever since.

The beach just south of St Ives is called Porthminster. Legends say there once was a chapel nearby where a holy person lived, though now no one knows where the chapel was. But at dusk, when the wind is north of west, you can sometimes see a small craft appear from round the headland. In the half-light the crew come ashore and haul the boat out of the water, then they kneel on the sand in a circle. They are dressed in dark cowls and cloaks and the men all are bearded. After a few minutes they climb the cliff. When they reach the top they turn right and head up towards Tregenna Castle before they are lost to sight. Some believe it's a vision of St Ive or her friends. Perhaps Tregenna was where Ive made her holy cell after sailing across from Ireland on her leaf.

In the west of Cornwall there are chapels and holy wells dedicated to Ive and her companions, so she obviously made a good impression among the Cornish people. But in those days a tyrant King ruled this part of Cornwall. Teudar was his name. He was a pagan; he hated immigrants in general, and Christian immigrants in particular. He couldn't abide the fact that Ive and her friends were persuading the Cornish to be good and peace-loving. So he sent out his soldiers and ambushed them, and everyone was put to death.

'Crumbs. They were rough times', said Jamie.

'True,' said Anthony, 'but in Cornwall then the Irish were better known as pirates, so you can imagine Teudar being wary of them. But I reckon he was a nasty piece of work. He also tried to kill Meriasek, the patron saint of Camborne. Meriasek was smart and he was never caught. But even he had to flee to Brittany. They may have been friendlier there!'

17

LELANT

South-east of St Ives, the pair trudged along the golden sands of Carbis Bay. At the end of the beach a headland projected into the ocean, so they briefly turned inland. On the headland they found a hovel. Working in the garden was a wild-eyed man. His forehead was bald, but his sideburns were unkempt and they joined with a curious and straggly beard from which a clean-shaven chin jutted. A cow and a pony stood in the next field. Round the man's hoe a black cat played. Seeing the pair approaching, this strange man stopped his work. 'Gardening's a thirsty business,' he said, 'would you care for tea?'

'Why, thank you sir,' said Anthony.

Then, to Jamie's horror, the old man, followed by his cat, pony and even the cow, all set off down the cliff on a dangerously steep path. Amazingly, none slipped. At the bottom the man filled a kettle, and the animals drank from a spring. He scrambled back up the cliff and soon the kettle was on the fire. 'Well now,' said the old man, 'my name's William Bottrell, what's yours?' Introductions over, they sat down round a simple table. Over tea it became clear that this curious man had a wealth of stories. 'I have earned and lost three fortunes,' he said, 'in Spain, in Canada, and in Australia. Now what I have is what you see and my memories.'

William Bottrell seemed fond of children and talked of the young people who visited him. He said to Jamie, 'It's too early for fruit, would you like a carrot?'

But mostly Bottrell talked of the tinners who worked in mines close by. 'You can see their tunnel entrances on the cliff', he said. 'They work underground all day, and still spend a couple of hours helping me clear the ground for my garden. Just in return for tea and company. I learn many tales from these tinners. They sit by the fire here and yarn whilst I take notes and sketch them. The tinners have intelligence, mother-wit and memories,' he said grandly, 'and I am able to garner from their ample harvest.'

THE KNOCKERS

The old miners all speak of the 'knockers'. They say that in the dark of the mine, far below the ground, they hear distant knocking sounds. Those are the sounds of the little people who live under the ground, working away with drills and hammers, picks and shovels. Some say they are the descendants of Jews doomed to work underground because they condemned Christ. Mind you, you won't find that in the Bible, just in superstitious minds. These little people are full of fun amongst themselves when unobserved, but much more sober in behaviour when spied upon, and they can be spiteful if you don't treat them right. You'll find them in caves, old wells and, of course, in mines.

It's always wise to leave the knockers something to eat; some heavy cake or a piece of pasty, maybe. And you should never swear or shout at them. To do so is foolish, for the knockers work only profitable grounds and they make themselves known only to those whom they favour.

BARKER'S KNEE

Once there lived a big hulk of a fellow called Barker. Now Barker would rather do anything than work, and he never believed anything people said. He had been told of a particular fairy well, but he said it was 'all a dream'. He didn't believe in piskeys, knockers or fairies at all. But as all the people around him believed in the fairies of the well, he said he would find out.

So day after day, Barker would lie among the ferns growing around the well and, basking in the sunshine, he listened and he watched. Soon he heard pick and shovel, conversation and merry laughter from deep underground. Day after day, week after week, Barker returned. He never saw a thing, but after a while he learned to make out the words used by the busy workers far under the ground. He discovered that each shift was eight hours long and, at the end of the shift, the little miners hid their tools.

Then one evening he heard one knocker say he was going to hide his tools in a cleft in the rock. Another said he would put his tools under the ferns. But finally another said he would leave his tools on Barker's knee. Barker was startled at hearing his own name and at that moment a heavy but invisible weight fell on his knee. He groaned in pain and shouted to have the cursed thing taken away. But all he heard in reply was laughter from the depths. From that moment to the day he died, Barker had a stiff knee. Sadly, he was laughed at by everyone in the parish. No one believed his tale, just as he had not believed them when they spoke about the knockers. From that day on 'Barker's knee' became a proverb: an excuse for any man who didn't want to work.

'And,' said William Bottrell, 'even if you did believe in the knockers you had to treat them right.'

TOM TREVORROW

On the cliffs near Land's End is Ballowal. The oldest mine in Cornwall, it was worked before Noah's flood! Down there your candle will show the green stain of copper, blue of nickel, red of iron, black of tin – a tear-filled rainbow on the granite. It's haunted by thousands of spirits. Not just knockers, but also ugly spriggans, who guard both the ore and the tools, and memories of miners long dead. It's enough to frighten the boldest miner. One such man was Tom Trevorrow, a miner from Trencrom who came to St Just looking for work. He got a job in Ballowal, and so did his eldest boy.

From the start, Tom could hear the knockers. Each day they seemed to be getting nearer; the noise of their tiny shovels and picks grew louder and louder. They became so loud that they started to irritate Tom. He realised that although he could not see them, they could see him. Whenever he made a clumsy stroke, their laughing and squeaking, which ordinarily was bad enough, grew much noisier. One day he lost his temper.

'Go away you old spirits!' he shouted, throwing a handful of broken stones down the tunnel, 'Or else I'll scat your brains out!' Straight away a shower of loose rock fell about him and scared him out of his wits. But Tom was a happy-go-lucky chap, so he shrugged his shoulders and went back to work. At mid-shift he sat down to eat his meal. There was silence as he ate his pastry cake or fuggan. But as he came to the last crumbs, he heard squeaky voices calling, 'Tom Trevorrow! Tom Trevorrow! Leave some of your fuggan for Bucca, or bad luck to you tomorrow!' But Tom ate the very last morsel. His candle was almost burnt out and suddenly he felt very sleepy. His eyes were heavy, his limbs very tired and he fell fast asleep.

When Tom awoke, the tunnel was dark and silent. In front of him were dozens of knockers, also resting. As he stirred, they all looked at him. They leered at him between their spindly shanks, thumbed their noses, squinted their eyes and pulled the most awful faces. Tom was very frightened so he lit another candle. To his relief the knockers vanished into the rock and he climbed up to the surface as fast as he could.

When Tom told his friends what had happened they shook their heads in dismay at his treatment of the knockers. But Tom was not one to worry about such things and next day he set off to the mine as cheerful as ever. But when he got there he saw that some timbering was about to give way. Tom and his boy repaired it in an hour or so, but he could hear the knockers working away close at hand. The two then decided to get some of their tin ore up to the surface. To do this, they had first to repair a small shaft and windlass. As Tom worked, he could hear the knockers hammering closer and closer. Then suddenly, the ground began to move beneath his feet. Tom started to fall into the shaft, but his son reached out, grabbed him and pulled him to safety. When Tom was able to calm himself, he saw that all the ore they had mined and all their tools had plunged down the shaft. It was a miracle that he had not been killed.

Tom's bad luck was a lesson for one and all. It lasted for years, and not just at Ballowal. He gave up mining altogether and become a farmer, but he still had bad luck. In the end, it was his wife who changed his luck. She visited a 'peller', a 'white witch' who at last broke the spell of the knockers.

18

Etek

GWITHIAN

It seemed to Jamie they had walked for hours over fine, soft sand. His legs ached. Anthony James trudged in Jamie's footsteps holding the string he used for guidance.

Anthony asked him, 'What colour is the sea?'

Jamie looked mystified, 'It's a sort of blue-grey colour. It would be called 'glas' in Cornish.'

'If you wanted,' said Anthony, 'you could take a swim. I'll wait on the sand.'

With a sigh of relief Jamie stripped off and swam in perfect waters from a perfect beach. Afterwards he asked, 'Why did you want to know the colour of the water?' Anthony replied, 'These waters can be beautiful. But ahead the Red River enters the sea. It carries mine waste from up by Redruth and Camborne. At Pednandrea the mine waste runs through the street. It's as if the blood of the mine is flowing past the miners' doors, and here is where it comes. If the wind and tide are wrong the sea is a soup of poison chemicals. Then no one should go swimming.'

They continued round the bay. Every so often Anthony would offer a word of encouragement. 'Of course, lots of people have been swallowed up by these sands.' Jamie was not impressed. Anthony continued, 'This is where the Lord of Penwith had his manor: he and his harpers and pipers and tabourers. Fine men all of them, I've no doubt. But now look, there's nothing but the sand dunes; towans they call them. But though the lord and his fine houses are long gone, the old stories survive. Jamie,' said Anthony, 'I want you to remember that.'

'Now Jamie,' he said, 'once there was a man who was a storyteller and a fiddler and a singer and a dreamer. The preacher told him that his fiddle played the music of the Devil and he was bound for hell. His wife said she would disown him if he continued his sinful ways. So he hid his fiddle away. But when the time was right he would go for long walks on his own. He would go to the very edge of the land, take out his fiddle, and play and sing to anyone or anything within earshot. He knew the tales and tunes would survive, but only if he helped them.'

On their left a cliff kept the sea at bay. At first the drop was just a few feet, but soon the path climbed steeply. Then, to Jamie's surprise, he heard the sound of a violin. The tune was unlike anything he had heard before. High, sustained notes fell to a low sigh; the phrase was repeated again and again.

'That'll be Old Bashty,' said Anthony, 'he don't look much, but in his own world he is one of the best. Mind you go careful now.' Looking ahead Jamie could see a figure silhouetted on the skyline. He was wearing a scruffy overcoat and a woollen hat was crammed on his head. The strange music stopped as the figure turned. Initially the man looked worried, as if he feared discovery, but then a smile of recognition creased his face.

'Anthony James!' exclaimed the figure, 'I thought you were dead and gone.'

'Not just yet,' said Anthony, 'though the Frenchies and the recruiting party had a good go at both of those. Bashty, this is young Jamie. He's my eyes these days, and he's a fiddler too.'

'How do you do, Jamie', said Old Bashty.

'Very well, sir,' said Jamie, 'but my feet are rather sore. Please, what was that tune you were playing?'

'Come here, boy', said Bashty. 'Careful, mind.'

Jamie caught his breath. As he took two paces forward he saw the ground ahead fall away hundreds of feet to a beach. The sands were protected on three sides by near vertical cliffs. He dropped to his knees to peer over the edge.

'What can you see?' asked Old Bashty.

'Sea, sand, rocks', said Jamie.

'Watch and wait,' instructed Old Bashty. He put his fiddle to his chin and started to play. Again came the sustained high note, then the sighing fall. Then again and again the phrase was repeated, echoing on the wind above the sound of the waves below.

'Now what can you see, boy?' he said.

'There's something in the water, it looks like a black boulder, but it's moving.'

'Good', said Old Bashty, and played on.

'There's another,' said Jamie, 'and another, and another. What are they; are they mermaids?'

It was Anthony James who spoke. 'They're seals. This is their favourite place. In the high summer they are out on the skerries or even as far as the Isles of Scilly. But the rest of the year, they come here. Under the cliff are great, secret caves where their babies are born. There the seal mothers sing to their pups, they love the music. And I bet they tell them stories too.'

Old Bashty played on and soon seals were clambering up the beach.

'This tune,' said Old Bashty, 'is the seals' own call. I play it when I sense it is time for the seals to gather.'

'And what do you do when they are gathered?' asked Jamie.

'Then,' said Old Bashty, 'the storytelling begins!' He looked down to the beach. 'But not today,' he continued, 'they can't wait to get out to the skerries.'

As soon as the music stopped the seals were returning to the water.

'Follow me, lad,' said Bashty, and set off along the cliff edge. 'Careful, mind!'

Old Bashty led the way, fiddle in hand. Jamie followed, pursued by Anthony holding onto his string. The cliffs grew ever higher and steeper; the waves seemed taller and louder. 'Up there,' cried Bashty, 'that's called Hell's Mouth. Ask any sailor and he'll tell you the same as the preacher: once you're in the jaws of hell there's no way out.' Then Old Bashty paused. He spoke with a kindly tone, 'Here, boy. Lie down on the cliff edge. Look down, here's something you'll not see very often.'

Jamie lay down and peered over the cliff edge. The drop seemed vertical and the sea was peppered with rocks, but immediately below was a deep pool. In it surfaced a young seal, then another appeared. Initially they faced each other, then one turned and zig-zagged away. The second seal followed as if playing tag. From his high vantage point Jamie could see deep into the clear water as they twisted and tumbled in the waves. After ten minutes they paused in the pool again. Briefly they faced each other. Then they set off once more, this time side by side, as if dancing together. The creatures that were lumbering and awkward on land were transformed into the most graceful things he had ever seen. Spellbound, Jamie watched the display. For another quarter of an hour the seals danced together, then again they paused in the clear water. It seemed that the wind and waves died away for a moment. Then Jamie heard a call from below. It was a high, keening note, sounding clear above wind and wave. Then came a sighing fall as the sound faded to nothing. Moments later the seals turned for the open sea.

19

Nownjek

PORTREATH

To the travellers, the village of Portreath seemed to be all confusion. The directions Anthony James gave to Jamie did not seem to relate to the streets and buildings. The descriptions the young lad gave his sightless guide triggered few memories in the older man. Where once had been a little fishing cove, masons were building a new harbour. Terraced cottages stood where once had been fields. A new tramway led uphill in the direction of Camborne. All the talk was of horseless carriages and Richard Trevithick's new steam engine which made the horse-drawn trams look as if they were standing still. All the change made Anthony feel insecure, as he relied on his memory of the past to construct his image of the present. But to Jamie it was the most exciting place he'd ever been.

As they arrived a band was marching through the town. Bugles blew, fifes whistled and drums banged; a crowd of excited children danced behind them. Jamie took out his fiddle to join in, but Anthony could not keep up. They stopped at the inn. One of the dancing children looked back, saw Jamie's fiddle, and skipped across.

'What's that?' she asked.

'F-fiddle,' stuttered Jamie, embarrassed and also surprised at the question. He put it to his chin and played.

'My dad's in the band', she volunteered. Then she skipped away, white stockings dancing in the sun. Jamie put away his fiddle and took out a turnip from his bag. As he nibbled, he was again inter-rogated, this time by a large lady.

'What do you call that?' she said.

'A turnip?' asked Jamie.

'Of course it's a turnip! Is that all you've eaten today?' Jamie nodded. 'Huh!' the lady slammed into the inn. 'Don't you move,' she shouted as she disappeared. She reappeared twenty minutes later. In each hand was a plate of bacon, eggs and bread. She thrust them at Anthony James and young Jamie. 'I'll not have travellers starving on my doorstep', she said.

Anthony James stood, doffed his cap, and gave a little bow. 'Thank you ma'am,' he said, aiming a kick at Jamie. 'Thank you', said the lad.

The band gave up when a steam hammer started operating down at the new harbour. One by one the children came back down the road. Anthony had a smile or a kindly word for every child, known to him only by their footfall or high-pitched voice. Gradually a small crowd gathered round Anthony and Jamie. The girl with white stockings was among them. Anthony and Jamie played some tunes, starting with 'The Girl I Left Behind Me' which was easily the most popular tune in Cornwall that year. Some adults joined them at the sound of the music, and then the stories began.

GIANT WRATH

It's a rough coast near Portreath, but it's safer now than it used to be. For long ago there lived a great giant; his name was Wrath. He used to have the bay to himself, which is why it used to be called Port Wrath. But when humans came he left the bay and went to live in a great cave called Wrath's Cupboard, just one mile west of the harbour. There he would lie in wait, watching for any vessel that came too close. If any ships or fishing boats were careless enough to come within a mile of his lair he would wade out, tap the sailors on the head to knock them out and then drag the ship into his cave. There he would eat the well-fed

*sailors, but the skinny ones he would throw back into the sea. They say
he kept the fattest to the last.*

*If a ship was too far offshore, so that Wrath could not wade out
in the deep water, he would stand on the cliff top and throw great
boulders at them. Do you know, at low water you can still see all those
boulders forming a great reef stretching out from Godrevy Head.*

There was a murmur of recognition among the listeners. Amongst
them were some fishwives in their traditional costume, with distinctive starched bonnets or gooks on their heads. 'Don't you
worry my dears,' reassured Anthony, 'old Wrath's long gone, and
the roof of his cupboard has fallen in. But sailors still call it "The
Giant's Zawn" to this very day.'

A voice piped up, 'Are there any other giants?' It was white-
stockings who spoke.

'Hundreds, to be sure,' said Anthony, 'each one bigger and hun-
grier than the one before. Mind you, they don't always win.'

GIANT BOLSTER

*About five miles north of Portreath there lived a great giant called
Bolster. He was so big he could stand with one foot on Carn Brea
and the other on Trevaunance Beacon. He and his wife giant marked
their land by building that great earth and stone bank that goes from
Trevaunance round to Chapel Porth – a gurgoe they called it in the old
days. But Bolster was a cruel giant and he gave his missus the hardest
job: carrying all the great boulders off the fields and piling them up on
the beacon, and they're still there to this day.*

*Now Bolster cared nothing for humans and he would often eat a
cow or a pig that strayed his way. He was so big no one dared argue
with him. The local people lived in fear and trembling; often they went
hungry. But they could not think how to get the giant to go away.
However, one day Bolster spied a pretty young Cornish maid and
although he was a married man he immediately started to court her.
Now this maid was brave and clever, so she played along with him,*

pretended she didn't mind. Bolster promised her the earth if she would live with him, but she said she needed proof of his love.

'Ask me anything,' said Bolster, 'I'll do anything to prove my love.'

'Would you give me something?' asked the maid.

'Whatever you want. Gold, silver, jewels; they're yours', said the giant.

'How about a tiny drop of blood? Just enough to fill this little hole on the cliff edge.'

'Easy', said Bolster, for compared to his great bulk the hole was tiny, the size of a thimble. So he stuck his knife into one of his veins to fill the hole.

But it wasn't just a thimble hole. It was what we call a pepper-hole or a spout. It had a tunnel leading into the sea. And so as fast as the giant's blood filled the hole, it drained away into the ocean. Eventually the giant let all his blood drain into the sea, and soon he was quite dead. The sea was red with blood for weeks after. In fact, they tell me that when the tide is right it is still red.

I'm told the maid's name was Agnes, perhaps even the holy woman of that name. That's why they call the headland St Agnes Head, 'cause she outwitted old Bolster and made the land safe for all her people. Nowadays the village is called St Agnes too.

'I think that's cruel', said white-stockings.

'Well he wasn't a very nice giant. He was married; he was cheating her', said Anthony.

'But she tricked him', said white stockings. 'She was no better than he was.'

'Sometimes,' said Anthony, 'the difference between saints and sinners is hard to find. What's your name, little girl?'

'Jenefer,' she said, 'it was my mum that gave you your meal.'

'Well,' said Anthony, 'I think you're lovely people.'

'So do I,' said Jamie, and played her a tune on his fiddle.

20

PERRANPORTH

The path along the cliff edge was as tiring as ever. Although the ocean seemed fairly flat, the coastal path had innumerable climbs and descents. But the day was clear, the sun bright and the sea was blue, which somehow made the miles less tiring. After a while a magnificent beach became visible – perhaps two miles of perfect sands shining gold in the afternoon sun. To the right was a fishing village. At the head of the cove was a rock with a tiny chapel on it. Beyond, magnificent lines of breakers swept in. The waves moved swiftly, so that long trails of spume flew from the crest of each wave, translucent in the sun. Jamie stood in awe of this magnificent sight. For a full five minutes the two travellers stood in silence. Then above the sound of the waves Jamie heard a sound; a plaintive tune could be heard played on a violin. On the cliff sat a bearded old man. He played the violin as if the sea was a concert audience, and the thunder of the breaking waves was the applause at the end of a masterwork. When the old crowder had finished Anthony James shook his hand.

'Tommy Trudgeon! Still playing then?' Anthony questioned the old man.

'When the breakers are high and the wind is offshore, like today', answered the fiddler. 'When it's like this I imagine old Piran coming ashore, his curragh surfing in on the waves.'

'What's a curragh?' asked Jamie.

'It's an Irish rowing boat', said Tommy. 'Some people say that Piran came from Ireland, though the truth is that no one really knows. All the place names associated with Piran are here in Cornwall. There's Perranporth, Piran's harbour; Peranzabuloe, Piran's church in the sands; and Perranwell. Piran could have been Irish, but it's more than likely he was a Cornishman. Perhaps he went to a seminary in Wales or Ireland and then came home. But either way, what a welcome to Cornwall – the golden sands of Perranporth on a bright, clear day!'

ST PIRAN DISCOVERS TIN

Mr Gilbert Davies at St Erth says that Piran is the saint of tinners, and his flag is a white cross on a black background. They say that the black part of the flag represents the cassiterite, the special black rock that has the tin locked inside, and the white is the silvery tin itself. The old tale is that Piran came ashore in his little boat. He was cold, tired and wet. The local people made him a shelter in the dunes; they brought firewood and made a small fireplace out of the local black stones. Soon the fire was blazing, they were singing songs and swapping stories. Then Piran noticed a silvery substance flowing from the rocks of the improvised hearth and realised it was tin. Ever since then, Piran has been the patron saint of tinners.

'It's a good tale,' said Anthony James, 'but they've dug for tin in Cornwall for about 3,000 years. They were doing it 1,500 years before the time of Piran!'

'What about the flag?' asked Jamie.

'Who knows?' answered Anthony. 'No one knows where Mr Gilbert got his information. At the battle of Agincourt, back in 1415, the Cornish fought under a banner showing two Cornish wrestlers. But a white cross on a black background is simple and distinctive, good things for a flag.'

The crowder said, 'I like the tale about Piran in Ireland.'

'So do I', said Anthony. So Tommy the old crowder began his tale.

THE COMING OF ST PIRAN

When Piran left the seminary he first worked in south-east Ireland. The people there were mostly pagan, as was the High King of those parts. I think the King's name was O'Connor, and he only just tolerated having Piran working in his land. Well one day the King decided that he was a deprived King. He only had seven wives, poor chap. Clearly this was quite inadequate, so he asked another seventeen ladies to marry him. Although he was rather bad-tempered, as he was the King they all agreed.

Well Piran might have been very holy, but he was not a good politician. When Piran heard about the King's extra wives, he made the error of preaching against the King from the pulpit one Sunday morning.

That morning, the King was in his magnificent castle having a sumptuous breakfast with his seven wives and seventeen fiancées. He was always grumpy at breakfast time, but when he heard what Piran had been saying he became even grumpier. The King decided to get rid of Piran.

At the very same time, Piran was sitting in his broken-down hovel, eating a very frugal breakfast all on his own. He realised it was going to be a bad day when two-dozen heavily armed soldiers joined him at the breakfast table. Well, they didn't so much join him as burst through the door. Then instead of sitting down to eat, they seized Piran and dragged him to the King's castle.

It's curious, isn't it, how the rich and powerful feel threatened by poor people who see the world through different eyes to theirs.

In his castle, the King declared that a public execution was to be the penalty for Piran's anti-establishment doctrines. So the King, with his seven wives, seventeen fiancées, household retinue, soldiers and the entire population marched to the top of the highest cliff in the land. Piran was tied to a millstone and rolled to the cliff edge. 'Do you have any last words?' he was asked.

'I can't swim!' he said.

The King replied that the rope and the millstone were just in case Piran learned to swim on the way down. With that they rolled the millstone over the edge of the cliff. It hurtled through the air and landed in the water with the biggest splash you can imagine. Like a tidal wave, it was.

But when Piran landed in the sea, because he was a holy man, the water became holy water. That great big splash soaked everyone on the shore. The King, with his seven wives, seventeen fiancées, household retinue, soldiers and the entire population were soaked with holy water and unexpectedly baptized on the spot.

Then the rope binding Piran said, 'This is a holy man, I should not be binding him', and all the knots untied themselves. Then the millstone dragging Piran below the surface said, 'This is a holy man, I should not be drowning him', and the millstone bobbed up and floated on the surface.

Then Piran stood up on the millstone and saw that the King, with his seven wives, seventeen fiancées, household retinue, guards, soldiers, flunkeys and the entire population were now Christian, having been very unexpectedly baptized. Piran realised that his work in Ireland was done and it was time to move on to bigger challenges. To the east was Cornwall! So Piran said goodbye to the King, with his seven wives, seventeen fiancées, household retinue, soldiers, and the entire population. Having been converted, they were now all very fond of Piran, so they wept bitter tears at Piran's departure. In fact, there were

so many tears it was like a waterfall and it caused a huge wave. So
Piran, still standing on his millstone, invented surfing and rode that
wave across the Celtic Sea until he reached Cornwall.

When he reached Cornwall, he made landfall at a magnificent
beach – two miles of perfect sands shining gold in the afternoon sun.
Magnificent lines of breakers swept in and long showers of spume flew
from the crest of each wave, translucent in the sun. To this day they call
the magic place he came ashore Perranporth.

Now when the sun lights the breakers, I always look to the west to
see if there is a lone figure on a millstone, longing to make landfall in
his homeland. I play my old violin. I may be few years late, but I still
want to play a 'Piran's Welcome'.

21

Onan Warn Ugens

St Columb &
St Breock

North of Crantock, they crossed the steep-sided River Gannel by a small ferry. The oarsman talked about the shipbuilding at the head of the river and the epic voyages of Gannel schooners, to Wales, Ireland and who knows where.

Next they passed a fishing village nestling by a small quay under the cliffs. 'Towan Blystra', announced Anthony. 'It's just a few small boats on the sands. But they are talking of making a new quay here, and then it will all be different!'

Then they followed the road east, through the bustling little town of St Columb. There, in the Red Lion, the landlord told them tales of Cornish wrestlers. 'The best known is Richard Parkyn. "The Great Parkyn" they call him. He lives up at Parkyn Shop where three parishes meet: St Columb Major, St Columb Minor and St Mawgan. He's so good that all three parishes claim him.'

'The landlord knows a lot about it', whispered Jamie.

Anthony replied, 'His name is James Polkinghorne; he's a fine wrestler himself, probably the only one that could take on Parkyn.'

Jamie looked at the barman. Then above the bar he noticed a silver ball with an inscription on it.

'The other thing they're keen on here is hurling,' said Anthony, 'village football. There's a match every Shrove Tuesday, using a famous silver ball. It's town folk against country folk, that's why the motto on the ball is "Town and country – Do your best!" People come from miles to see the fun. The goals are two miles apart and no one knows the rules. You have as many people on each side as you want. You can kick, throw or run with the ball, whatever you like.'

'It sounds like a riot,' said Jamie.

'You could say that!' said Anthony. 'But they still say "Gware wheag yeo gware teag", which means "Fair play is good play!"'

Next morning Anthony and young Jamie found themselves in a steep-sided valley on the edge of the hills above Wadebridge. There a rush of trees sheltered from the wind that whistled across the moor and a swift stream danced between them. Deep among the trees was a church, well shaded by beech and yew. There was no one else around, but to Anthony James it was full of life.

'This is St Breock, I know it by the sound of the stream', he announced. Whimsically he added, 'Good stream, floods the church every year! Saves 'em mopping the flagstones. Jamie,' he said, 'the door is round the side – you must lead me. They all used to come here', he volunteered.

'Who was that?' asked Jamie.

'Morris dancers,' was the reply, 'every year they came from miles around to St Breock. One side even walked from Ludgvan, down by Penzance; that's a good forty miles each way.'

'That's a long way to come for a dance.'

'Yes, but there were plays and wrestling and hurling and all sorts of fun. Each village had its own dance, it was a matter of pride to come to St Breock. But they don't come any more.'

'Here's the door', said Jamie, and they went inside.

'Now then, Jamie, lead me up the right-hand aisle until we're near the wall.' The two figures stopped at the eastern end of the church. Anthony spoke again, 'Can you see anything on the wall?'

'There are old slate memorials,' said Jamie, 'to the Tregeagle family.'

With some satisfaction Anthony announced, 'This is the Tregeagle aisle.'

Said Jamie, 'Two generations of Tregeagles are mentioned here.'

'But not three. Can you see a Jan Tregeagle mentioned?'

'No,' said Jamie, ' I can see John and John and Joan, but no Jan.'

That's right', said Anthony, 'There's some say that Jan Tregeagle is buried out in the churchyard, and there's some do say he's not.'

'But surely they know?' asked Jamie.

'The register says he was buried here,' said Anthony, 'but no one knows where, and some say that even if you find his grave, it might be empty.'

'Empty?' asked Jamie. His innocent eyes looked up into Anthony's sightless face, and his guide started to speak.

JAN TREGEAGLE

Jan Tregeagle was estate manager to Lord Robartes. Jan was a giant of a man, a crook and a bully. The tenants hated him, and with good reason. He was the sort of man that went into a farm for a dozen eggs but always came out with thirteen because he cracked one. He was forever making life hard for the tenants, and if they didn't watch him like a hawk he'd cheat them of their rent.

He was so evil some said he sold his soul to the Devil. No one grieved when he died and was buried in St Breock churchyard. There may even have been some celebration. But that was the beginning of the trouble. There had been so much cooking of the books that no one knew what had been going on.

Now Robartes was a lord and spent lots of his time up in London, doing whatever lords do. But he was a good man, so he came down from London to sort things out. He sat himself down at a great table and one by one he heard all the tenants who had been treated unfairly and made it up with each of them. At last there was just one farmer left, and he was an honest, church-going man. According to the ledger he owed a month's rent. But the farmer put his hand on the Bible and said, 'I swear to God I paid this rent. I can only imagine that Tregeagle

put the money in his own pocket. May Jan Tregeagle himself come here and tell us the truth!'

There was a thunderclap and the room grew midnight black. When it grew light again, there was Jan Tregeagle. He looked alive and quite well, if slightly singed. Robartes made him put his hand on the Bible and promise to tell the truth. Then Tregeagle admitted that the farmer had paid the rent, but no entry had been made in the receipt book for he had indeed put the money in his own pocket.

So it seemed that the matter was closed, and Robartes told Tregeagle he could leave. But that was when Jan Tregeagle said, 'No! I'm not goin' back where I just come from. Old Nick, he's waiting for me there with his trident and his hell-hounds and his fires. And Saint Peter won't let me into heaven 'cause of all I've done. So I'm not moving.'

'You can't stay here', said Robartes. 'You're supposed to be dead!'

'I don't care,' said Jan, 'I'm not goin' anywhere.'

It was a stalemate. No one knew what should be done. So Robartes sent for the Abbot of Bodmin. In those days the Abbot of Bodmin was the wisest and holiest man around; he still carried the holy bell of St Petroc. And the abbot decided that as long as Tregeagle worked for those he had wronged, he could remain on this earth. If he stopped, Tregeagle would have to go back to hell.

The abbot gave Tregeagle the job of emptying the Dozmary Pool on Bodmin Moor. That pool was always flooding the cottages nearby. But the Dozmary Pool is bottomless, and to empty it Jan Tregeagle was given just a limpet shell. To cap it all, the shell had a hole in it. It was such a tiresome job that he groaned and wailed as he worked away. And some of those groans and wails were so heartfelt they stayed on the wind. So if you go up there on a night when the wind is blowing, they say you can still hear him groaning as he struggles to empty the pool.

Now the Devil felt cheated. He had lost a soul from hell. So he tried to distract Tregeagle, stop him working, and so take him back to down to stoke the eternal fires. On the first night the Devil sent a great gale.

The wind tore at Jan's clothes and tugged at his arms. But Jan kept working away. On the second night the Devil sent rain and thunder and lightning from the end of his trident. But nothing could distract Tregeagle from his task.

But then on the third night the Devil sent his hell-hounds. They barked and bayed and snapped and slavered, but Jan kept on bailing. Then one leapt high enough to knock the limpet shell from Tregeagle's hand. As it fell he grabbed it with the other hand. He caught it! But it was wet and slippery, and it fell through his fingers into the water. He grabbed again and missed, and it sank into the bottomless pool.

Tregeagle was now fair game for the Devil. The hell-hounds rushed towards him and he fled for his soul across the moor. He ran all the way over past Bodmin. There's still a hill there called Hellman Tor. The locals say some of those hounds got lost up on the Tor; sometimes you can still hear them baying. But no one knows if they're calling for the Devil, or still looking for someone to take down to hell, and I don't suppose anyone's going to find out.

At last Tregeagle reached a hermitage on top of a pillar of rock by the village of Roche. 'Sanctuary, I crave', he cried. It was sacred ground so the hounds could not touch him.

But the hermit was fed every day by his daughter, who used to carry provisions up from Roche village. With the hounds snarling and snapping all round she couldn't get to the hermitage. And the baying of the hounds was too much for the local people, it kept them awake at night. So again they sent for the Abbot of Bodmin. Well, of course, the hounds fled at the first sight of his crozier and the first sound of his holy bell.

The abbot heard that Tregeagle had done his best to empty the pool. So instead of being sent to hell, Tregeagle was given a new task, carrying sand and stones away from the beach below Berepper across to beyond Porth Levan. But one dark night the Devil sent his demons to distract Tregeagle. One demon managed to trip Tregeagle, so he stumbled and dropped the sand and stones he was carrying and they fell across the mouth of the Cober River. At one time big ships could nearly sail to Helston, but this dam created the Loe Pool and stopped ships sailing up the river, and it was the end of Helston as a great seaport.

Of course Treageagle was then given yet another job – weaving rope from the sands of the Doom Bar at Padstow, to try and make it a safer place for sailors and fishermen.

Padstodians will tell you that Tregeagle is still there. Every night he weaves a good length, but then the tide comes in and washes it away. Groaning and wailing he has to start all over again. For all I know he is still living in a cave below the cliffs at Stepper Point, just by the Doom Bar. To prove me wrong someone would have to find and open his grave at St Breock to see if it is empty, and no one has ever been brave enough to do that. So the morris men don't come here any more, in case they should meet Jan Tregeagle visiting his old haunts. In the meantime, it's as well to be careful if you're on your own up on the cliffs near Stepper. You never know who you might meet there. It might be old Jan looking for a soul to send to hell in his place!

The funny thing about the stories of Jan Tregeagle is that the further west you go, the bigger Jan gets, and the stories get taller too! Up by Bodmin he's about six foot six inches. By the time you get to the Lizard he's miles high and has a bird's nest in his beard!

22

LITTLE PETHERICK

That night Anthony and young Jamie played and sang and told tall stories at the great rectory up above St Breock Church. The rector was a jolly man and together they laughed and sang the night away. The two travellers slept in the servants' quarters and were well fed. Next morning the sun was at their back as they made their way up over the edge of the high ground. Soon they were on an old trackway. In places it had been worn deep into the ground by countless pairs of feet. Jamie spoke first. 'Lots of people must have come this way before us', he said.

'Indeed,' said Anthony, 'But many would have been travelling the opposite direction to us. The first one I know of was St Sampson. He came from Wales and landed down at Padstow. Then he walked across to Fowey. I expect he stopped at Bodmin on the way, to meet up with his holy friends.'

'Like the abbot', added Jamie.

'Like the abbot,' said Anthony, 'and all the rest. Bodmin means "dwelling of the monks" in Cornish. Of course in those days most people here spoke Cornish, though the priests and educated people would all have spoken Latin as well. But Cornish is very like Welsh, which is why St Sampson and the other Welsh saints got on so well when they came to Cornwall.'

The old track led though farms and hamlets, then down into a steep valley. At the foot of the valley, by the stream, was a mill. Crossing a picturesque bridge Jamie could see open water to the north. 'That's the Padstow Estuary', said Anthony. A little higher up the hill stood an old church, rather in need of repair.

'St Petroc,' read Jamie, 'is this Padstow?'

'I'm afraid we still have three miles to go,' answered Anthony, 'but you're thinking well. St Petroc is indeed the church of Padstow; once it was called Petrockstow. But Petroc also had another, smaller, church a few miles to the east. It was called Little Petroc, now they call it Little Petherick. That's where we are now.'

'So there are churches named after Petroc in Bodmin, Padstow, and here in Little Petherick', said Jamie.

'That's right,' said Anthony, 'and many others too. Cornishmen quite rightly celebrate St Michael and St Piran. But Petroc was undoubtedly the greatest saint of medieval Cornwall. In the tenth and eleventh centuries, when Cornwall had its own diocese, it was officially under the patronage of St Petroc and St Germans. Every year thousands of pilgrims used to come to St Petroc's at Bodmin.'

'So Cornwall really does have three patron saints?' asked Jamie.

'At least three!' laughed Anthony.

ST PETROC, THE SERPENT AND THE DRAGON

Petroc loved animals. When he arrived in Cornwall, he found that for miles around Padstow people were terrorized by a giant serpent. So he went out to the headland where it usually appeared. As soon as it saw him it came slithering out of the sea as if to gobble him up. But Petroc held up his staff and sounded his holy bell. 'In the name of the strong power of the Trinity, you will stop', said Petroc to the serpent.

Straight away the serpent became docile and let Petroc place his stole gently around the serpent's neck. Then Petroc quietly ordered the serpent to remain far out in the ocean and hunt fish, not humans. With his stole he led the giant serpent to the water's edge. Then he gave the serpent a blessing and bade it farewell, and it swam off into the ocean and never troubled the people of Cornwall again.

On another occasion, one morning when Petroc came out of his little cell here in this valley, he found a dragon waiting outside. He politely asked it to go away, which it did, but next morning there it was again. Once again he politely asked it to go away, and again it left, but on the third morning there it was again. So he asked the dragon what it wanted, but the dragon just wept. So Petroc bravely went close to the dragon and then he saw it had a splinter in one eye. It had heard of Petroc's reputation and had come to him to be healed. So Petroc took out the splinter and bathed the eye with holy water until it was healed. Then the dragon bowed its thanks and flew away, never to be seen again.

PETROC AND CONSTANTINE

One day, when Petroc was an old man, he was walking in the wood here in this valley. It was a favourite place of his, very peaceful. All of a sudden a little deer ran up to him for protection, only a young thing it was. It was being chased by three hunters with bows and arrows. Petroc held up his hand and called out, 'I'll have no killing on holy ground. Be on your way brothers, go in peace.'

Then the chief hunter shouted back, 'Deer are the royal prerogative! Stand aside, old man, or I'll kill you too. I am Constantine, Prince of Cornwall. This is my land, I hunt where I will.' Then he took an arrow from his quiver, and placed it on his bow. Now Constantine was already known to be a contentious and immoral character. The famous St Gildas had rebuked Constantine, but then had to flee to Brittany to save his life.

'In the name of the strong power of the Trinity, you will stop', said Petroc to Constantine.

'Not I; stand aside!' said the Prince and started to draw back his bowstring. But then Petroc held up his staff and sounded his holy bell, and in that moment the young Prince was rooted to the spot. Constantine could not move, his body was wracked with pain and he cried out in agony.

Then Constantine shouted to his men, 'Quick, kill the deer and the old man too!' But Petroc just looked them in the eye and shook his head. They faltered and looked at the Prince, who was still immobile. They saw the pain on Constantine's face and they were too scared to do anything. While they stood there the fawn ran safely into the forest.

'When was the last time you were in church?' asked Petroc.

The Prince was silent, for the last time he was in church was an occasion when he had disguised himself as a clergyman so he could pursue some enemies.

'Well then, my friend,' said Petroc, 'let us speak for a while.'

Then Petroc undid the spell and Constantine rather sheepishly put away his bow and arrow. Petroc explained to Constantine what he needed to do to mend his ways and live a good life. And I'm pleased to tell you that Constantine took Petroc's advice and became a great leader. Constantine gave Petroc an ivory hunting horn as a token of thanks and recognition of his sound advice. Eventually Constantine became a holy man himself. He founded the monastery at Bodmin. He also built himself a little chapel by the sea, and now they call that place Constantine Bay. Later people built a church there, named after him, but it was swallowed by the sands. But Constantine's old holy well, that's still there and the water is always pure.

From that day onwards Petroc was loved by all animals because he had protected one of their own, and he was loved by the Cornish people, for he had given their leader wisdom and understanding.

'That must have been a long time ago', said Jamie.

'It was,' said Anthony, 'a very long time ago.'

23

Trei Warn Ugens

ST ERVAN

TRAVELLERS

On the far horizon they could see St Eval Church, its prominent tower whitewashed by the merchants of Bristol so it would be a navigation mark for ships heading for the Bristol Channel. After a while, in the narrow lanes south of Padstow, Anthony and Jamie reached a crossroads. 'This is gypsy corner', announced Anthony. There the hedges, all of good Cornish stone, fell back from the road and there was an open green space. Against the hedge on the windward side were several improvised tents. Ponies grazed at the roadside. Children played and well sunburned adults sat at a fire. On the steps of a caravan a pretty woman held a baby. Jamie described the scene to his Anthony.

'Take me to them', he said.

'Is that you, Billy Orchard?' Anthony cried out. One of the men by the fire stood and spoke.

'Anthony! Devlesa avilan.'

Anthony James replied, 'Billy, devlesa araklam tume!'

Jamie looked on uncomprehending. Anthony spoke to him, 'This is Billy Orchard and his family. Billy is a traveller, a Romany. Some say he's hard, but if you show a bit of manners, like you would for anyone else, you'll find he's one of the best. What he just said was "It is God who brought you" and I replied "It is with God that I found you." But that's about all the Romany I know.'

'Where are you going, Billy?' asked Anthony, for travellers are always going somewhere.

'St Ervan; the Glebe', said Billy. 'The rector is one of the best. The Prebendary they call him. He looks stern, but he says we are all God's children. He prays for our dead, marries our couples and baptizes our children. Others aren't so kind. So we come to St Ervan every year. We camp on his land and we work on the Glebe. Some of my lads are working there right now. Then when his harvest is home then he gives us a fine harvest supper, guldise he calls it.'

That evening they walked down the lane and then took a narrow path through thick brambles and blackthorn. Soon they were walking by a small, man-made waterway. After a while, the sound of splashing, running water increased and Jamie saw the water was channelled onto an overshot water wheel. Jamie described the scene to Anthony. 'This is Millingworth', he said. 'In Cornish it means "Higher Mill". It has been the chief mill for the parish for centuries.'

They crossed the mill stream by a narrow, stone clapper bridge. The stone slabs looked as if they too had been there for centuries. Then the lane climbed steeply. They paused to drink at a spring hidden beside the path.

'This is what the locals call St Ervan's well. Now it provides water for Millingworth, but the locals will tell you it was used by the saint himself. They still use the water for baptisms.'

Above the well stood the old church. In it Jamie found the registers. Under 'baptisms' they found the name Orchard many times. On each occasion, in the rector's neat handwriting, the father's profession was described as 'Egyptian.' 'It means traveller, gypsy,' said Anthony, 'some people think that travelling people originally came from Egypt.'

CRYING THE NECK AND GULDIZE

Close by the church was the rectory and the Glebe Farm. They could hear voices from the field nearby, and followed the sound.

There the oldest of the harvesters slowly and steadily swung his long-handled scythe, or 'zwy' as he called it, and felled the last of the standing wheat. Then he deftly twisted a handful of stalks around the middle of the bundle to gather it together and lifted it above his head. In turn he faced east, south and west.

Each time he called out, 'I have'n, I have'n, I have'n!'

Then the assembled crowd shouted back, 'What 'ave ee? What 'ave ee? What 'ave ee?'

'A Neck! A Neck! A Neck!' he replied, and everyone cheered.

Then the rector led the way to the Glebe Barn, where supper was waiting. 'In the old days they used to call the harvest feast "guldize",' remarked Anthony, 'it's Cornish for "Feast of the Hay Ricks".' Ale was served in pitchers and soon the music and dancing began. Every song seemed to be about the harvest. There was 'John Barleycorn' and 'The Barley Mow'. Then there was a shout for 'Old Mrs Davey' and a jolly lady stood up and started to sing:

Sow one for the rook and one for the crow,
one to rot and one to grow.

To Jamie's surprise a girl leapt to her feet, seized a besom and started to dance in time with the song. He could see that the dance acted out the tasks of clearing of the weeds, sowing the seeds and gathering and threshing the corn. Soon everyone was dancing as

Anthony and Jamie played their fiddles. First it was a three-hand reel. This time everyone sang:

Some say the Devil's dead and buried in Fowey harbour.
Some say he's alive again and prentice to a barber!

Then came a four-hand reel and then even a six-hand reel, the dancers spinning and twining in figures of eight on the barn floor. Then, with everyone weary, someone cried out, 'A droll, a droll! Give us a droll', and Anthony started to tell his tales.

St Ervan, the Merchant and the Beggar

Now there was none so wise in all the land as old St Ervan. He was always being asked to settle disputes of one sort or another.

Well once there was a poor travelling man. He'd been on the road for days and no one had shown him any kindness at all, so he was very hungry. This travelling man came walking down the very lane that runs outside this barton. It just so happened that in those days there was a merchant in the village who was very wealthy. He always had plenty to eat and he always seemed to have lots of friends. It's funny, it often seems that way. Anyway it was supper time and the merchant and his friends were just about to sit down to a magnificent meal. There was beef and pork and spuds and greens with thick gravy, and apple pie and clotted cream as well. The aroma was wonderful.

Just then, who should come by but the poor travelling man, and he smelled that most wonderful aroma coming out of the merchant's door. It was the best thing he had smelled in days, so he paused to savour it. Just then, the merchant looked out of his window and there he saw the ragged old traveller. The merchant rushed outside and shouted, 'Get on your way, you dirty old traveller. You can't stand there. You'll frighten my guests.'

'But this is the King's highway,' said the traveller. 'I'm doing no harm; I'm only savouring the aroma of your very fine supper.'

'Well, it has cost me good money to buy and prepare this supper. If you're savouring the fruit of my labours you must pay for it!' said the merchant.

'Don't be daft!' said the traveller, 'Anyway, I have no money.'

'Pay,' said the merchant, 'or I'll have you locked up!'

'I will not!' said the traveller.

Then both men looked round because they heard footsteps, and there was good old St Ervan walking down the lane.

'Aha,' said the merchant, 'you're well known for solving disputes. This traveller is savouring the aroma of my supper and won't pay for it. Make a judgment will you. This supper has cost me a lot. Tell him how much he should pay. He should pay up or move on!'

St Ervan thought for a moment then he said, 'Do you happen to have any silver coins in your purse?'

'Of course', said the merchant.

'Please could I borrow a handful?' said St Ervan.

'Oh all right,' said the merchant, 'but why don't you just get on with it? Tell this vagabond to pay up or move on.'

St Ervan let the silver coins fall from one hand to another so they clinked together as they fell. 'Did you hear that?' he asked.

'Yes,' said the merchant, quite exasperated, 'but what about your judgement?'

'My judgement is this,' said St Ervan, 'that the value of the smell of your supper, is that of the sound of your silver. Merchant, as you eat your fine supper, think on those less fortunate than you. Traveller, go to the Glebe Farm, where you'll find kinder, gentler folks.'

They are still there to this very day!

24

Pajar Warn Ugens

CONSTANTINE BAY

Not far from St Ervan, the travellers found themselves wandering across a wide sweep of sand dunes. In the distance, Jamie could see another headland and he could hear the roar of the sea.

'This is Constantine Common', said Anthony. 'Do you remember about King Constantine?' he asked Jamie.

'The King who became a holy man?' asked Jamie in return.

'That's him!' said Anthony, 'After Constantine was converted by St Petroc he built his cell somewhere around here, but no one knows exactly where because it's long been lost under the sands. Then in medieval times they built a church here that was dedicated to him. But the sand started to bury that too. For a while they used the building as a poorhouse, but it was no use. The people tried to keep the dunes at bay, but the sand overwhelmed the old church. It was piling up against the walls, breaking down the doors and windows. So they took away the font and the slates and the roof beams and the carved stones and used them to help make a new church at St Merryn, just up the road. But there are some folk around who will tell you that Constantine is still here to this day. He has the shape of a barn owl, but he still watches over the ruins of his old church.'

'But back-along some of the locals started hearing strange noises and seeing flickering lights, and they realised that the place was haunted. The field next to the church, maybe it was once the old churchyard, was said to be a piskey field and no one much would go near the place after that.'

'No one at all?' asked Jamie.

'Well,' said Anthony, 'there was one.'

PISKEY LED

The Edwards family were shepherds who farmed on Harlyn and Constantine Commons. Old William Edwards lived over by Harlyn in a rented cottage. The rent for the cottage was a pie. The pie had to contain limpets, raisins and herbs, and William had to present this pie every year on the feast of St Constantine.

Now one feast day, after paying his pie-rent, William joined the celebrations in the Farmers' Arms at St Merryn. Sadly, William was a man who was fond of a drop or two. Apparently there was a storyteller in the Farmers' Arms that night, spinning yarns about old Constantine and about the piskeys and so on. Old William had so much fun that he stayed very late indeed. When he left the inn he set off towards Harlyn, but he hadn't been going long when he reckoned he could save a bit of time by cutting across the sand dunes on Constantine Common.

After a while, William reached a five-bar gate and he realised it was on one side of the piskey field. On the far side of the field was another gate, and beyond that was the lane leading to Harlyn and so to William's cottage.

So William went through the first gate. Now it just happened that it was a night when there was no moon. But William could just make out the hedge in the starlight, so he reckoned he would be all right because he could follow the hedge round the field until he came to the gate on the far side. Well, he walked and he walked but he never found the gate. He walked and walked some more, but then he found himself back where he started.

Then William thought to himself, 'Maybe I wasn't paying attention. Maybe I was looking the other way when I passed the gate.' So he set off again following the hedge round the field. Once again he walked and he walked. Once again he never found the gate, but after walking for what seemed an age, he again found himself back where he started.

William was just beginning to realise that he had been piskey led when his eye was caught by a flickering light across the field. He walked towards it, thinking that it might guide his way. Soon William was looking over the hedge and beyond it he could see the outline of the old church of St Constantine. The ruins were lit by an eerie, flickering light. Inside the old church William could see there were piskeys and spriggans and knockers, all dancing away with Bucca himself playing on the old Cornish double chanter pipes. They started with a three-hand reel, then a Cornish six-hand reel. The dancing was so good that William wanted nothing more than to join in. So he scrambled over the hedge and peered in at the window. 'Let's have another set,' he cried, 'and I'll show you a step or two.'

Then instantly all was silent. Bucca looked towards him with his eyes blazing red. He said, 'Show us a step or two? Do you think you are quick enough for that?' Then all the piskeys and spriggans and knockers came charging towards him. Straight away William realised that he was in mortal peril. He ran for all he was worth, but the spriggans were getting closer and closer.

Then suddenly in the darkness William stumbled and tumbled. There was a huge splash. He was full of panic, for he thought the spriggans would surely have him. In an instant his life flashed before him. He wept at the thought of never seeing his cottage again, of never again tasting limpet and raisin pie, or supping beer in the Farmers' Arms. But when he looked up there was not one piskey in sight. He had fallen into the old holy well of St Constantine, where no strange creatures ever dared to go.

William struggled up out of the well. He was wet through and shivered with the cold, such was the shock of his sudden baptism. He took off his jacket and wrung the water out of it. Then he put it on back

to front and inside out, for that is sure to confuse any piskey. Feeling
rather sorry for himself, he made his way home, water squelching in his
boots all the way. As he trudged the last few weary yards to his house
he heard a barn owl calling, and do you know, it almost seemed that
it was laughing.

The old holy well is still there. St Merryners say that to bathe in the
holy well will bring rain in dry weather. The remains of the church are
still there too, and so is the Farmers' Arms. But there is an old saying,
'Piskey led is often whisky led!'

25

Pemp Warn Ugens

PADSTOW

It was only a short walk to the sheltered port of Padstow. There everyone seemed most kind and convivial. Between the cottages clustered round the little harbour, in first one inn then another, Anthony and Jamie played and sang and they were well rewarded with fish pie. In the Golden Lion they were joined by a lively man called Caleb Boney. He talked about clocks and bells and pianos, and it was clear that although self-taught he was a very clever man. Also he played the fiddle very well and seemed to know the latest and most fashionable dance tunes. 'They do like 'un up at Place you know!' he said, conspiratorially. 'Mistress Frances, she plays all they tunes on her new piano!' When the music was over, that night they slept in a stable behind the Golden Lion.

At six o'clock in the morning, as the first light entered the room, Anthony was woken by Jamie's insistent voice. 'Anthony! There's a great black monster in the corner. We must leave before it wakes up.'

Anthony held the frightened lad close. 'Don't worry', he said. 'When I first saw it I was impressed as well. Just you stay close by me, and I'll tell you about it later.'

After an hour or so Jamie could see the monster more clearly. 'It's the 'Obby 'Oss', said Anthony. 'To welcome in the summer it comes out every May Day and dances round the town. Next year

I'll bring you here to see it all happen. I remember the first time I slept in this shed. Let me tell you what it was like…'

THE PADSTOW 'OBBY 'OSS

Early on May Day the first light crept into the room. As the shadows lifted, the dawn light gave life to the circular frame and its gleaming black tarpaulin cover. At the front was a little horse's head with snappers for jaws. The eyes shone and looked expectantly towards the door. At the back was a tail, and the moving shadows seemed to give it life. The rising sun revealed red and white ribbons decorating the rim, head and tail. The 'Obby 'Oss was ready.

After about an hour a small group of men came in. Two of them wore suits of white sailcloth. They were musicians: one carried a fife, the other had a drum. A third man carried a musket. Another carried a short club on which were written the letters 'O B'. Others went to the 'Obby 'Oss in the corner. They lifted it up and one man climbed under the frame and his head protruded through a hole in the middle. On his head they placed a fearsome black, white and red mask. It was unlike anything seen anywhere else in the land. It seemed powerful and strange, as if it came from another world.

Outside a voice started to sing. 'Unite and Unite' it began. The 'Oss and its followers went outside. Immediately the 'Oss began a wild dance, leaping and posturing, running and turning. The 'Oss was led by the man with the club, the teazer they called him. Every so often the 'Oss would collapse as if dead as the music slowed to a lament. Then it would leap into life once more and continue its dance as the music resumed a vigorous march time. It was exciting, frightening, and full of the vitality of the new summer.

The 'Oss went all round the town. It took a 'drink' in the harbour, it chased some sailors up the rigging of their ship.

At the maypole, and in other places too, the musket was fired. 'To ward off evil spirits', they said!

Occasionally a girl would be pursued and, if cornered, would disappear under the skirts of the 'Oss, emerging tar-smudged but laughing. Then they walked up to Prideaux Place, where Mr Prideaux emptied a purse into the hands of the party. Then on to the vicarage and finally to a farm called Treator, where the 'Oss drank from a pool. The farmer gave everyone ale and cheese, and there was dancing in the lane. Then the 'Oss went back down into the town and the revelry continued. At sunset it disappeared, as if by magic. The 'Oss had given its all to the new summer.

Later that day, high on the cliffs, Jamie and Anthony sat in the sunshine. They looked north-east across the estuary on the headland on the far side. 'The headland over there is called Pentire', said Anthony. '"Penn" is Cornish for head; "Tir" means land; Pentire. The headland this side is Stepper Point. Once it was called Starboard Point; it was on the starboard side of ships entering the estuary.'

'The cliffs are dangerous', observed Jamie. 'They could do with a lighthouse or day mark to help the sailors make a good landfall.'

'True,' said Anthony, 'but not all sailors making landfall here were friendly. Vikings raided the town, which is why they moved St Petroc's priory inland to Bodmin, and nothing's changed since then.

THE 'OSS, THE PETTICOATS AND THE SPANIARDS

The cliffs are the castle walls of Cornwall. The cliffs north of Padstow are where the womenfolk saved the town. Just like the wizard Merlin prophesied, in 1595 four Spanish galleons came and sacked and burned Paul, Penzance and Newlyn. But the Spanish were deterred from attacking Penryn, so the next place they went was Padstow.

Now Cornishmen in general and Padstow men in particular have always been renowned as great sailors. So at that time all the men of

Padstow were at sea with the likes of Grenville and Drake. Padstow seemed completely undefended. The Spaniards could have just sailed up the estuary and into the port.

But the women of the town were not to be defeated. First they put on their red petticoats. Then they took the 'Obby 'Oss and danced up on the cliffs at Stepper Point. The Spaniards had never seen anything like it. From out at sea they thought it was the Devil himself with a troop of redcoats. The idea that the Padstow was defended by soldiers who were in league with the Devil frightened them so much that they sailed back to Spain. So Padstow was saved by its maids, their petticoats and the 'Obby 'Oss!

'Padstow maids sound pretty resolute', said Jamie.

'They're pretty and they're resolute all right', said Anthony. 'They all have the spirit of the mermaid of Padstow. Sailing in and out of Padstow was never easy, but the sailors were always guided by a beautiful mermaid. All was well until the day that the Doom Bar was made.'

'What happened?' asked Jamie.

THE MERMAID OF PADSTOW

There once was an unfortunate chap called Tristram Bird. Padstodians say he was a visiting sailor, and visitors say he was a Padstow landsman. But now it doesn't matter, because it's all long past. Anyway, Tristram didn't seem to have too many friends and he wasn't at all successful with the young ladies of the town. Then one day he went and bought a gun. Perhaps he got it to impress people; he was forever showing off and bragging about what he was going to shoot with that gun of his. People got quite fed up, and the local lasses all laughed at him. So he went off in a huff. He walked out of the town towards the sea, past St Saviour's Point and round to Hawker's Cove. And there in the cove he saw the most shapely girl that he had ever seen. She was sitting on the edge of a rock pool, and she was looking at her reflection in the pool as she combed her hair. Tristram too could see the reflection of her face in the still water. He thought hers was the most beautiful face he'd ever seen. She was even lovelier than the girls of Padstow.

'Good morning,' he said, 'your beautiful face has quite bewitched me.'

'I'm afraid you are easily bewitched', she laughed.

'Your hair is the colour of golden corn', said Tristan.

'But not on your scythe', she shook her head.

He frowned, 'I have a fine house, with linen and crockery, just waiting for you.'

'I would not follow you if your house were full of silks and gold', she said.

'But how can you refuse a fine chap like me? I could marry one of a dozen Padstow girls.'

'Then why don't you ask them?' she questioned.

'Because I love you', said Tristram.

'How can you love me?' she said, 'You've only just met me. You don't know me. And don't I have any say in the matter?'

'You must love me,' said Tristram, 'and if I can't have you, no one else shall. I will shoot you.'

'Shoot me if you will, but marry you I will not', she said. 'But I warn you, if you harm me you will rue the deed for all eternity. I will curse you and this harbour that I have protected for so long.'

'I care nothing for your curses or your protection, they are meaningless', said Tristram. 'If I can't have you living, I'll see you dead.'

Then the foolish man pulled the trigger and shot the girl. As she fell she cried out the most terrible curse on both Tristram Bird and on the port of Padstow. As she died she rolled over and Tristram could see that below her waist was a graceful fish's tail. He realised with horror he had shot a mermaid and her curse was bound to be true.

He ran back to Padstow, weeping and wailing. When questioned, he told what he had done. If people teased him before, now they hated him, for to kill a mermaid is the most terrible thing. He was shunned for the rest of his days and, of course, never again did the mermaid guide ships in and out of Padstow.

That night the wind started to blow. A great storm rose up. For one, two, three days it blew. It was the greatest storm Padstow had ever known. Once the deepwater channel used to run close inshore by Hawker's Cove. But when the storm was over the sailors of Padstow found that channel had vanished. A great sand bar stretched across the estuary, so ships could only pass at high tide, and even then they were in great danger. Every year a dozen ships are lost on the Doom Bar, and they say it is the vengeance of the mermaid of Padstow. To this very day there is a rock pool down by Hawker's Cove that they still call the Mermaid's Glass.

26

TINTAGEL

Jamie had expected the castle to be grand but it seemed rather broken down.

'What do you expect?' asked Anthony, 'You'd look the worse for wear after 500 years!'

Jamie looked mystified. 'But I thought King Arthur was 1,300 years ago?'

'Quite right,' said Anthony, 'but the castle you can see was not Arthur's. This castle was built by the Earls of Cornwall in medieval times, just because Tintagel was King Arthur's legendary birth-place. Arthur was not born in this castle. But he might have been conceived here in another castle that disappeared long ago.' Jamie looked rather disappointed. 'I'm sorry,' said Anthony, 'let me tell you the story anyway.'

THE BIRTH OF KING ARTHUR

Many years ago there was a great warrior called Uther Pendragon. He defended his lands bravely and defeated all his enemies, so he was acknowledged as the High-King of Britain. In those days, Britain comprised many small, independent principalities; one of them was Cornwall. The Duke of Cornwall was called Gorlois and his castle was at Tintagel, an impregnable castle on an island on the north coast.

Once there was a council of war between Gorlois and Uther Pendragon. But at that meeting Gorlois was accompanied by his lovely wife, Igraine. As soon as Uther Pendragon saw the beautiful Igraine, he fell in love with her and resolved to have her for his own. However, she refused his advances. At the same time, Gorlois noticed that Uther was attracted to his wife, and so took her back to Cornwall straight away. Uther summoned Gorlois again, but he refused to come.

Now Uther Pendragon had a trusted advisor, Merlin the Magician. Merlin was the greatest magician that ever there was. So Uther told Merlin to invent a plan to enable him to get what he wanted.

So it was that Gorlois found his lands being invaded by Uther's army. Following Merlin's advice, Uther's men did not attack Tintagel. Instead, they attacked another Cornish castle called Dimelioc; some say it's now called St Dennis. So Gorlois rushed to defend Dimelioc, leaving Igraine at Tintagel.

Then, while Gorlois was busy defending Dimelioc, Merlin cast a magic spell on Uther Pendragon; the spell made Uther look just like Gorlois. Using this disguise, Uther made his way into Tintagel Castle unhindered and there he seduced the lovely Igraine. That night their son, the future King Arthur, was conceived. On the next day, over at Dimelioc, Gorlois was killed in battle and not long after Uther and Igraine became husband and wife.

When they found that Igraine was going to have a child, Merlin warned them that the birth should be kept a secret and the child should be hidden away.

Soon a healthy baby boy was born and he was christened Arthur. The child was bound in a cloth of gold and was secretly taken by two knights and two ladies to the back gate of the castle and given to Merlin, who was disguised as a pauper. Merlin carried little Arthur to a trusted knight called Sir Ector, whose wife brought up Arthur as her own.

Within two years, just as Merlin had feared, Uther Pendragon became ill and died. His lands were overrun by thieves, wicked knights and Saxon invaders from the east. If they had known of the birth of Arthur then the child would surely have been murdered. But because of Merlin's

*advice none of the tyrants knew about the boy and in safety Arthur grew
to manhood. What happened then, as they say, is another story.*

*There are many tales of how Arthur and his knights had twelve
great victories defending Britain against the Saxons. The stories are
found wherever the old British language was spoken: Cornwall, Wales,
Brittany and southern Scotland. Most of the places mentioned cannot
now be identified. But we can prove that those tales were known in
Cornwall before Geoffrey of Monmouth wrote them down. There are
many tales that told how the alliance of the Round Table broke down,
and they concern Cornwall as well.*

EXCALIBUR

*It is said that Arthur's last battle was in Cornwall. While Arthur was
fighting overseas he gave his jealous nephew, Mordred, the Lordship
of Britain. But when Arthur returned he found that his lovely wife,
Guinevere, had been abducted by Mordred. Mordred also refused to
give back the crown. They fought many battles, but Mordred made his
last stand in Cornwall at a place called Camlann. There, after a day
of fighting, Arthur killed the treacherous Mordred, but was himself
mortally wounded. It was the end of the day, but it could have been the
end of the world. The landscape was barren; all around lay the dead
and dying.*

Arthur summoned his old companion, Sir Bedivere, and

*commanded him to throw the sword
Excalibur into an enchanted lake nearby.
The lake was as dark as the oncoming night
and was said to be infinitely deep. Bedivere
took the sword to the water's edge. But the
sword gleamed like ice in moonlight, and
Bedivere could not bear to throw away such
a precious thing, so he hid the sword in the
reeds. When he returned Arthur asked him,
'Did you throw the sword into the lake?'*
'Oh yes', said Bedivere.

'What happened then?' said Arthur.

'Nothing', said Bedivere.

'You have not told the truth!' said Arthur, 'For a second time I command you, throw the sword into the lake.'

Again Bedivere took the sword to the lakeside, but the sword gleamed like gold in firelight. Again he could not bear to throw the sword away, so again he hid it. When he returned Arthur asked again, 'Did you throw the sword into the lake?'

'Oh yes', said Bedivere.

'What happened then?' said Arthur.

'Nothing', said Bedivere.

'You have not told the truth!' said Arthur, 'For a third time I command you, throw the sword into the lake.'

Again Bedivere took Excalibur to the water's edge. This time he summoned up all his strength and threw the sword high into the air. By now it was sunset. As the sword curved through the air, at its highest point it caught the last rays of the sun. The silver cross gleamed against the black sky. As the sword fell towards the lake a lady's arm clad in white samite appeared from the water. The hand caught the sword by the hilt, then carried it below without a ripple. So the Lady of the Lake took back Excalibur. Bedivere told Arthur what had happened; Arthur knew that this time he was telling the truth.

Then Bedivere heard the sound of keening, and as darkness engulfed the world, four fair maidens carried Arthur in a magic boat across the shining sea to Avalon. In human form, he was never seen again.

Some think that Camelford and the River Camel are linked with Camelot, and Camlann was at nearby Slaughterbridge. The Dozemary Pool is said to be where the Lady of the Lake took back Excalibur. Arthur's castle of Kelliwic could be Callywith or Kellybury. On Bodmin Moor are Arthur's Downs, Arthur's Hall and Arthur's Bed. Arthurian names like Merlin, Mordred, Tristan, Geraint and Erbyn are found in the Cornish landscape. The links between Cornwall and Arthur are old and strong, just like the granite land itself. And, mark my words, Arthur will return.

27

Seyth Warn Ugens

BOSCASTLE

North-east of Tintagel, the coastline had many dramatic headlands with rocky bays between. There was little shelter and it was clearly a dangerous coast, especially for small craft. After a while the travellers descended into a steep valley. There they found a tiny port. The approach from the sea twisted and turned through rugged cliffs. Small whitewashed cottages clung to the cliff side. It was very picturesque.

'This is Boscastle', announced Anthony. 'Once it was called Bottreaux's Castle. There was a mighty duke of that name who had a castle just up the valley. He used to have his own pipers. The river is the Valency. The name is from the Cornish for mill house', said Anthony. 'But the harbour has a reputation. If the swell is high, or the wind is in the wrong direction, it needs good seamanship to enter or leave safely, and sometimes a bit a luck as well. The entrance to the harbour is guarded by the Lion Rock. Near sunset the silhouette of the cliffs looks like a great, crouching beast.' In the harbour were many small fishing boats.

'How do the fishermen make a living in such a dangerous place?' asked Jamie.

'They charm the wind', said Anthony James.

'How on earth do they do that?' Jamie replied.

'If the weather is bad, or the wind direction is not good, then sailors will buy a wind-charm from a local witch. The witches of Boscastle have always been famous. Perhaps it was because their services were much needed in such a tricky harbour and on such a hazardous coastline. But perhaps it was also because they were good at their job.'

'Aren't witches bad?' asked Jamie.

'They have a bad reputation,' said Anthony, 'but most of that comes from the seventeenth century. Many people were persecuted then: Jews, Catholics, even Quakers. An evil man called Hopkins proclaimed himself Witchfinder General. He went on superstition and prejudice against anyone that looked, acted or thought different. Hopkins persecuted many people as witches, especially old women. But eventually people realised he was worse than the witches he claimed to find. Parliament and even some brave clergymen denounced him. He died in ignominy, but not before he had killed many harmless people. Some people still have wild ideas about witches, mostly based on old prejudice.'

ANNE JEFFERIES

Something over a hundred years ago, there was a lass, Anne Jefferies,
who lived not far from here at St Teath. A poor lass, but very bright,
she was apprenticed to a local farmer. One day when she was sitting in
the garden, six piskeys all clad in green hopped over the hedge. When
she saw them she had a fit, but from that day she could see piskeys
everywhere, even though they were invisible to everyone else. Once her
friends saw her dancing in the orchard. She looked quite alone, but she
said she was dancing with the piskeys. The piskeys taught her cures for
all manner of illness, and told her what would happen in the future.

One harvest time the farmer's wife went to the mill to fetch grain
so she could bake bread for the harvesters. But on the way home she
fell and hurt her leg so badly they sent to Bodmin for the doctor. Anne
insisted on seeing the poor wife and cured her just by gently stroking
her leg. From that day people came from miles around. Anne cured
dozens of people, but never took a penny from them. She went to
church regularly and never hurt a soul. But because she said she spoke
to piskeys, they put her in Bodmin Gaol for six months. They said it
must be the work of the Devil.

'It still happens. There's a "wise woman" in Bodmin – Joan Wytte
– I hear that she's been locked up too. There are many white
witches in Cornwall. People who know traditional remedies, signs
in nature, signs in the weather. Often they are called "pellers". Do
you remember the story of Lutey and the mermaid? Lutey and his
family were pellers.'

'So how do you make a wind charm?' asked Jamie.

'I'm no expert,' said Anthony, 'but this is what the long-liners
told me when I was a lad. The witch goes up to a high, windswept
place like Lion Rock. There they tie a special sailor's knot into a
stout piece of rope to capture the wind. You can capture different
winds if you tie your knots when the wind comes from different
directions or blows with different strengths. Usually three knots are
tied in the charm, and each knot has a wind of different strength.
Then the rope is sold to a sailor, and he unties the knots when he

wants particular winds. But you should never untie all three knots at once, for you never know what might happen!'

'Does it work?' asked Jamie.

'All I can say is that the witches here are still selling wind-charms, so I expect they are doing something right, or at least the sailors think they are!'

Anthony continued, 'Just remember, Jamie, no one knows everything, and most people are frightened of what they don't know. But as there are so many things in this world we don't understand, it's not unusual to find someone who knows something different to yourself. You never know, you might learn something from them.'

Then they headed for the high moorland that beckoned from the east. The afternoon sun cast a soft, gold light on the granite tors. In his mind's eye, Jamie saw a figure on every one, busy catching the winds from all over Cornwall, and each wind carrying a story or a song.

28

Eth Warn Ugens

ROUGH TOR

Anthony and Jamie had climbed high on the moors above Camelford. Jamie was concerned that Anthony wanted to be led up to the highest, rockiest peaks. It seemed laborious and dangerous. 'It's fine as long as you take your time', said Anthony. 'If you have time you can achieve anything.' Eventually they rested on what seemed the summit of Cornwall. All around were massive boulders, piled high on the summit plateau.

Anthony turned to face first one way then another. It almost seemed that his sightless eyes could see the magnificent view. 'This is called Rowtor', he said. 'From here you can see old cairns, stone circles, standing stones, farms, barns and fields that have been worked for three thousand years. But Rowtor is the hill with the story. You see the great slabs of granite on top of the hill? I'll tell you how they got here.'

KING MARK AND THE MOON

Many years ago Mark was the King of Cornwall. He was a very good King and he ruled very wisely, and he was respected by all his subjects. When it was nearly his sixtieth birthday, but not quite, his chamberlain came to him.

'King,' he said, 'you have ruled wisely
and well for many years. To celebrate your
birthday your subjects would like to offer
you whatever you desire. What is your
wish?'

The King thought for a while. 'Thank
you,' he said, 'there is one secret wish that I
have. I would like to touch the moon.'

So that night King Mark, his chamberlain and all his court walked
up to the top of Rowtor and waited till the moon appeared. As the
moon came sailing past, the King reached out and he could almost
touch it, but not quite.

The chamberlain commanded that the King's great dining table
should be brought from his castle. So his servants brought the table
and struggled with it up to the top of Rowtor. Then King Mark stood
on the table on top of Rowtor and waited till the moon appeared. As
the moon came sailing past, the King reached out and he could almost
touch it, but not quite.

Then the chamberlain commanded that every table in the land be
brought to the summit. All the citizens struggled to bring the tables to
the summit of Rowtor. There the tables were piled on top of each other.
King Mark stood on the topmost table on top of Rowtor and waited till
the moon appeared. As the moon came sailing past, the King reached
out and he could almost touch it, but not quite.

Then the chamberlain commanded that the King's throne be
brought to the summit. So his servants struggled to bring the throne to
the summit of Rowtor. There the throne was placed on top of the great
pile of tables. King Mark stood on the throne on the topmost table on
top of Rowtor and waited till the moon appeared. As the moon came
sailing past, the King reached out and he could almost touch it, but
not quite.

Then the chamberlain commanded that every chair in the land be
brought to the summit. All the citizens struggled to bring the chairs to
the summit of Rowtor. There the chairs were piled on top of the King's
throne. King Mark stood on the topmost chair on top of the throne,
on top of all the tables on top of Rowtor and waited till the moon

appeared. As the moon came sailing past the King reached out and he could almost touch it, but not quite.

'What is to be done?' cried King Mark, 'there are no more tables and no more chairs.' The chamberlain had no answer and neither did any of the court. It seemed that the King's secret wish could not be granted. King Mark called out, 'The one who can grant my wish can be my successor.' But it seemed that no one could solve the problem.

But there was a pageboy, the King's own nephew. His name was Tristan and he had a little footstool.

'I can help', said the pageboy and he handed up his footstool.

Then the footstool was placed on top of the pile of chairs. King Mark stood on the footstool on the topmost chair on top of the throne, on top of all the tables on top of Rowtor and waited till the moon appeared. As the moon came sailing past the King reached out and he could almost touch it. So he stretched and, 'Hurrah' they all cried, he caught hold of one of the horns of the moon as it went past. He quickly swung up a leg and sat on the moon and went sailing across the sky. Next night as the moon went sailing past they saw his smiling face looking down. Then they called up to the King, 'Is it true that the moon is made of cream cheese?'

King Mark replied, 'On the moon what look like seas are Cornish clotted cream, and what look like hills are Cornish china clay. And as I fly round the world, when I look down I can see Cornish men and women everywhere, for they are all valiant miners and bal maidens. Wherever there is tin or copper to be found there is a hard rock mine, and in every one I can see my fellow Cornish men and women.'

That is why the man in the moon is always smiling. On the top of Rowtor the tables and chairs are still there, though after all these years they are turned to stone!

'Jamie,' said Anthony James, 'I can't do it, but you can. You're young enough to reach out and touch the moon.'

29

Naw Warn Ugens

MORWENSTOW

The two companions were walking in the high-sided lanes of North Cornwall when they met a young clergyman. He was flamboyantly dressed in a claret-coloured coat, a blue fisherman's jersey, long sea-boots, a pink brimless hat and a poncho made from a yellow horse blanket. He was striding along the lane singing a song. The tune was similar to 'Auld Lang Syne' but the words were very different. Jamie remembered the chorus, 'Twenty thousand Cornishmen will know the reason why!'

'This,' whispered Anthony, 'must be Parson Hawker; a bit eccentric maybe. Do you know he once excommunicated his cat for mousing on a Sunday! And he has a pet pig. But he is a good, kind man. And he's a poet too. He has a hut up on the cliff edge, and there he writes his verses and watches for shipwrecks.'

'Surely this is one of the most remote parts of the country?' said Jamie, trying to make conversation.

'Oh yes', said Parson Hawker. The lane eventually led to a steep and rocky cliff.

'Surely this is one of the wildest coastlines in the country?' said Jamie.

'Oh yes', said the parson. 'The fishermen still say:

From Padstow Point to Hartland Height,
'Tis a watery grave by day and by night.

'They could do with a lighthouse or two on this coast', he added.

The coastal path led to the village of Morwenstow. Jamie was surprised at the worryingly large graveyard and mentioned it to Hawker. 'Oh yes', said the parson. 'For most of the souls laid to rest here are not those of peaceful villagers, but of poor sailors who met an untimely end on this dangerous coast. Sadly I must tell you that not all of them found their way there by the natural action of wind and wave. Even in this day and age there are still wreckers on the coast of Cornwall.'

Then Parson Hawker told this story. It was the most frightening that Jamie had ever heard.

MORGAN OF MELHUACH

One of the most notorious wreckers on the coast of Cornwall was Gilbert Morgan, who lived near Melhuach Cove. His name was linked to many wrecks, but nothing was ever proven. He was always there or thereabouts, but never caught in the act.

One autumn night Morgan's beacon lured a fine, black barque into the cove. Soon she was pounded by the surf and rolled to her destruction by the breakers. And there on the shingle was Gilbert Morgan, collecting the cargo as it floated in. Then, to his horror, in the starlight he saw a figure stumbling ashore. It was the navigator of the ship. Not only was he the only survivor, but the only one apart from Morgan who could know the truth of the shipwreck.

Morgan did not hesitate, but plunged into the wild surf, waded out to the half-drowned man and helped him up the beach. Near the head of the cove was a hollow in the shingle. 'Rest here,' said Gilbert, 'I will fetch help.'

The poor sailor lay down. But then Gilbert Morgan did not go for help. Instead he put a great boulder on the sailor's chest so he could not move. Then Morgan heaped shingle onto him until he was completely buried. They say that as Gilbert went on collecting the flotsam he could still hear the man's pitiful cries above the noise of the storm. That is, until the tide came in. Then there was an awful, awful silence.

Years later, Gilbert Morgan was on his deathbed. He had no friends, but neighbours watched over him. It was a fierce night. The wind howled and the waves lashed the shore. Morgan seemed to be delirious. He kept shouting out, 'He was already dead when I buried him. He was already dead, I swear.' Clearly he was terrified, but of what no one could imagine.

At the same time, watchers on the cliff top saw a great black barque sail into the cove. They heard the sound of the anchor chain in the hawse pipe as the anchor was lowered. Faintly they could hear voices calling, but for whom they did not know. 'Your berth is ready, your time has come, we must catch the tide before the dawn.'

In his cottage, Morgan was close to death. At the last he gave another great cry of fear, 'He was already dead, I swear.' Then Gilbert Morgan passed away.

From the cliff top the watchers saw a bedraggled, frightened figure being led onto the deck of the ship. They saw a hatch being lifted. For a few seconds the sails were lit with a red glow, as if a great fire was burning in the hold. They heard a scream of terror as the shaking figure was led below forever.

Then the sky seemed to lighten. They heard a distant capstan shanty as the anchor was raised. A halliard shanty echoed as the sails were hoisted and the black ship sailed straight out to sea, right into the eye of the wind. It was never seen again.

If you go to Melhuach Cove when an onshore wind pounds the breakers ashore, you can still hear the cries of Gilbert Morgan above the sound of the waves as he is led to a fate that is truly worse than death. But then again, perhaps they are the cries of one who is still buried in the shingle and who knows the tide is coming in.

Parson Hawker left waving a cheery goodbye that seemed rather out of place given the story he had just related.

'That was terrifying', said Jamie.

'It is indeed', said Anthony. 'It's a story I'm very wary of. As storytellers it's our job to take our listeners on impossible journeys, but we must always bring them safely home again. I'm not certain that the story of Gilbert Morgan brings any listener safely home, though I suppose in the end it was the villain got his come-uppance.'

'Shall I tell you a secret?' he continued.

'Yes please,' said Jamie.

'It is true that the Morwenstow wreckers have a bad reputation. It is said that they would not take the hand of a drowning man. But there's no such place as Melhuach Cove and there was no such person as Gilbert Morgan. But, south of Padstow, the most notorious gangs of wreckers in the land are at Mawgan Porth and Constantine Bay. And the leader of the Mawgan Porth wreckers is an evil man called Melhuish. I reckon that Parson Hawker swapped the names over just to keep himself out of trouble!'

30

Deg Warn Ugens

EASTCOTT CROSS

One day the two companions were in the farthest north of Cornwall. In the warm afternoon sun they rested high on the moors. Above them the buzzards circled slowly in the blue sky. On the hillside Jamie dozed on a rock. He looked so relaxed and it seemed that he had been sleeping peacefully, but when Jamie woke his eyes were wide as he stared about him.

'What is it Jamie?' asked Anthony, as he reached out a comforting hand.

'I had the strangest dream', replied Jamie. 'I dreamed of here, this very place. I dreamed I saw a beautiful girl sitting on a rock. But she was weeping, weeping as if bereft, beyond consolation. Then when I woke I recognised about me the scenery of my dream, but there was no girl. Just a rock on the hillside, and below it a stream flowing into a crystal clear lake, and below that a young river flowing south towards the sea.'

Anthony smiled, 'You have dreamed well. I'll tell you the rest of the story.'

THE LEGEND OF TAMARA

Once there was a bad-tempered troll who lived high up on the moors in the north of Cornwall. This troll had a beautiful daughter called Tamara. Now this old troll hated the light, so he slept during the day and would only venture out of his cave at night time. And Tamara, she was forbidden to go out during the day and only allowed out after sunset. But you'll soon learn about young women! You will find they are independent and inquisitive, just like many other people, perhaps more so. Well, Tamara was like that. One bright day, when her father was fast asleep, she crept out of the cave just to see what it was like.

As soon as she came out of the cave she was enchanted by the bright light, the colours, the reflections. There was the blue of the sky, the brilliance of the sun, the rich green of the moors, the silver streams and the sparkling, shimmering sea. And on the side of the hill there she found two young giants enjoying a friendly wrestling match, and I can tell you she was even more enchanted by these two strong, handsome young men.

And those two young men were friendly and courteous. They introduced themselves as Davy and Terry, and Tamara enjoyed their merry wit and their good company. She was fascinated by their knowledge of the world that lay beyond her close horizons. So next day she joined them again, and the next day, and the day after. And gradually she realised she was falling in love, not only with her young giants, but with life outside the cave, life in the light.

One day Tamara was sitting in the sunshine on the hillside between her two young friends. She was wondering which, if either, she preferred when she heard a howl of rage. She looked towards the entrance of the cave and there was her father. The old troll had woken and found that his daughter was gone. From the shadows of the cave

entrance he ordered Tamara to come back to the darkness at once. Tamara looked at the dark cave and her angry father. Then she looked at the bright land outside the cave and the two genial giants. Finally, weeping with fear, Tamara refused to do what the old troll said. Then her father's rage was so great that he was almost incapable of speech. Finally, screaming with anger, he uttered a great curse in a tongue no one else could understand.

Then Tamara felt her blood run cold and her limbs become stiff. Tears began to flow from her eyes as she realised that the curse was turning her to stone. Soon she was a lifeless rock, but from that rock the tears still flowed. At the base of the rock formed a pool of tears, tears that flowed forever, forming first a brook, then a stream, then a river that flowed down to the sea.

Then Davy cried out for the bad-tempered old troll to undo his terrible curse. At first the troll refused. Davy was insistent. But then the troll admitted that the curse could not be undone. So Davy drew himself to his full height and demanded that he too should be cursed, so that he could suffer the same fate as his sweetheart and share her course to the sea. So for a second time, and now himself trembling with fear, the troll uttered his great curse. Then Davy too felt his blood run cold and his limbs become stiff. Tears flowed from Davy's eyes as he was turned to stone by the troll's curse. From that stone the tears continued to flow. At the base of the rock formed a pool of tears, tears that flowed forever, forming first a brook, then a stream, then a river that flowed down to the sea; a river that joined with his beloved Tamara and flowed with her to the sea, far away to the south.

Then Terry roamed the hills seeking solace or diversion. But, wherever he went, he was haunted by the memories of his brother and his friend. Eventually from far across the moors he gave a great cry, demanding that he too should share the same fate. And far away the old troll heard his cry borne on the wind and for the last time uttered his terrible curse. In turn Terry heard the troll's faint words on the wind. Soon Terry felt his blood run cold and his limbs become stiff. Tears flowed from his eyes as the third curse turned him to granite; a stone that like the others wept an eternity of tears. At the base of the rock formed a pool of tears, tears that flowed forever, forming first a *brook, then a stream, then a river. But he was far away across the moors, so his river did not flow to the south and join Tamara and Davy. Instead his river flowed to the north, eventually joining the Bristol Channel.*

That's how the granite kingdom of old Cornwall defined its borderlands – three curses, three tears and three rivers: the Tamar, the Tavy, and the Torridge. That's what they call them now.

'Goodness, is that true?' asked Jamie.

'I doubt it,' said Anthony, 'but, mind you, all my tales have at least a little bit of truth.'

'I know', said Jamie, 'Beware those who live for darkness!'

'Right', said Anthony. 'And another moral of the tale is to do your young people the courtesy of letting them make their own decisions. Which way do you think we should go next?'

31

Udnek Warn Ugens

MINIONS

Late one evening they found themselves still walking as the sun set. They had played for the mistress of Rillaton Manor and then had eaten at the inn in Rilla Mill, snug in the deep and wooded valley of the River Lynher, one of the tributaries of the Tamar. To the south and west the sunset etched the high skyline of Caradon Moor as sharp as if it had been cut with a knife. But then they crossed the river heading south-west. Jamie would have happily watched the river for a while and perhaps tried some fishing before staying the night in the valley. But Anthony seemed careless of the time of day and walked briskly up the hill with Jamie propelled before him as a guide in the narrow, high-sided lane. Soon it was dark, but despite Jamie's heartfelt protests they marched on upwards. They passed the hamlet of Upton Cross, never pausing. Soon Anthony felt the south-westerly breeze on his cheek and his steps became less laboured; both factors told him he was now high on the moors of Caradon.

On the very top of the moor, in the shelter of a rocky outcrop, they boiled a kettle for tea and ate bread and cheese. When the meal was over Anthony commanded, 'Put the fire out Jamie, so there's not even a glow.'

Anthony heard the boy kick the sticks apart and stamp out the embers. 'Right,' he said, 'close your eyes and don't open them until

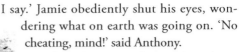

I say.' Jamie obediently shut his eyes, wondering what on earth was going on. 'No cheating, mind!' said Anthony.

After what seemed an age, Anthony said, 'That's long enough. You can open your eyes now. Look up.' Jamie looked up and gasped at the widest, brightest night sky he had ever known. There were so many stars, and they were so bright they seemed nearer than ever before. Anthony said, 'Tonight there's no moon and up here the air is clear. This is the best view of the stars you will ever get.'

Anthony asked Jamie to describe the patterns the stars made. Stargazing with a blind guide was not easy, but gradually Jamie was able to pick out the Plough and Orion and Cassiopeia, and a very bright object that might have been Jupiter. Anthony told tales of Orion the hunter. 'The sky is full of stories', he said.

Next morning dawned clear and cold as the sun rose over Caradon Hill. As Jamie awoke he was amazed to find he had slept in the shelter of an amazing pile of rocks that was narrower at the bottom than the top. Anthony explained that this strange tor was called the Cheesewring, and the uppermost stone spun round whenever it heard the cock crow. But even this unlikely information was ignored when, in the growing daylight, Jamie noticed orderly circles of standing stones on the open moorland. One or two stones were missing from the pattern, but it was clear the arrangement was man-made.

'They are the Hurlers,' said Anthony. 'Do you remember hurling, the village football they play at St Columb and in St Ives?'

THE LEGEND OF THE HURLERS

One Saturday up on Caradon Moor they had the greatest hurling match the land had ever known. Now the local priest, it must have been St Cleer I suppose, warned them about being finished before the

Sunday, that being the holy day. Well they played their hurling all Saturday, but the match was not over. So to get finished they continued on the Sabbath day. Some will tell you it was the Devil himself persuaded them. On the Sunday night they finished the hurling when it got dark, of course. But that was when the fun started. They persuaded two pipers

to come and play for them and they started dancing. So there were the pipers blowing away and three rings of dancers were leaping and skipping for all they were worth. Every one of them was heedless of the warning they had been given.

But that night there was a great storm with thunder and lightning and mist and cloud. In the morning there was no sign of the hurlers and no sound from the moor. So the local people went up there to see what had happened. There they found that every one of the hurlers had been turned to stone. And if you look away to the west you can still see the two pipers as well. Not one of them escaped and they are still here, to this very day.

Jamie gazed at the stones. 'That seems a bit severe', he said. 'Turned to stone for having fun?'

'Well,' said Anthony, 'perhaps they were turned to stone for being disrespectful to the Almighty, which is a bit different.'

'All the same…' said Jamie thoughtfully.

'I'm afraid some religious people are like that', said Anthony. 'Keener on retribution than forgiveness. Makes you wonder if they read the New Testament at all, and it says more about them than their religion. Furthermore,' Anthony continued, 'they say that if you count the stones twice and get the same answer each time, then something nasty will happen to you! Do you want to try it?' Jamie looked at the petrified figures on the moor. 'I don't think I'll bother, thank you!' he said.

LONG TOM OF MINIONS

As they walked south towards the valley of the River Fowey, they passed another standing stone. 'That'll be Long Tom!' said Anthony.

He used to be the best poacher hereabouts. Some say he concealed his activity by getting a job as a gamekeeper! But he was always boasting of his skill and word got around. Eventually his reputation reached all the way to hell. One night the Devil challenged Tom to a contest, to see who could take most lives during one night. If Tom won he was to have untold riches; if he lost then his soul was forfeit. Well all night long old Tom worked away, snaring rabbits in every warren, even catching the odd deer. He was doing really well and at dawn he had more than he could carry. Then the Devil appeared, and he was empty handed.

Tom started to laugh. 'I've won!' he shouted, 'You've got nothing at all.'

'Listen', said the Devil. Tom listened, and on every side he could hear distant weeping and wailing.

'Tom,' said the Devil, 'this night I have brought the plague to Cornwall, and taken more lives than you could claim in a century of poaching. You are coming with me!'

When the villagers next came that way there was no sign of Long Tom, but where he normally stood to survey the moor there was a standing stone. To this day people will tell you it is none other than Long Tom of Minions.

St Neot

On the south side of the moor Anthony and Jamie joined the old drove road heading towards Bodmin. Its shadows were alive with the memories of generations of travellers. Soon the pair crossed the River Fowey and that afternoon reached St Neot, the old church dominating the village.

'Who was St Neot?' asked Jamie.

'They say he was a Cornishman who lived about the time of Alfred the Great. Apparently he was once a soldier, which is curious because they also say he was only four feet tall. If both those statements are true, he must have been a particularly fierce fighter! But he gave up soldiering to live in a monastery. Some say he was a sacristan at Glastonbury. But some way or other he finished up back in Cornwall where he started out. Apparently he was a very kind man who looked after the poor when times were hard. We could do with a few like him I reckon.'

ST NEOT AND THE FISHES

By the St Neot River is a holy well dedicated to St Neot; the water there is supposed to be able to cure people. Old Neot used to stand in it every day and recite psalms. You'd have thought he would have caught his death of cold!

Well, one day St Neot found he had nothing left in his larder. So, as he stood in his well, in between the psalms he prayed that some good fortune would come his way. That very night he had a dream. An angel appeared and told him to look in the well, but to be sure never to take more than one of anything that he found there.

So next day St Neot went to the well and looked in it. There he saw three fishes. He could easily have caught all three, but he remembered what the angel said. He just caught one of them and had it for his supper.

Then on the next day he went to the well again and looked in. To his surprise there he again saw three fishes. He could easily have caught all three, but he remembered what the angel said. He just caught one and had it for his supper.

So it was the next day and so it was every day. Each day he caught one fish, and the next day when he returned there were always three fishes in the well.

Then one day St Neot fell sick; perhaps he caught a cold after all! He was getting weaker and weaker. His friends brought him medicines, potions, special foods and treats but he got worse and yet worse. Then his servant, Barius his name was, remembered that his master always liked fish from the well, so he decided to give his master some fish. Barius went to the well and there he saw three fishes. He caught all three of them and took them to St Neot for his supper.

But then St Neot declared that one was enough, and the lesson was that we should never take more than we need. So he told Barius to put two of the fishes back in the well, which he did. The very next day St Neot was restored to health. When he looked in the well he saw the two fishes had been miraculously returned to life and, furthermore, another had appeared. So once again there were three fishes in the well of St Neot.

ST NEOT AND THE DEER

St Neot always got on well with animals. Once, thieves stole the oxen from his monastery so he had no way of drawing the plough, making the furrows or sowing his seed corn. So St Neot said a prayer and deer came out of the forest to pull the plough. So it was that St Neot sowed his crop and the thieves were so impressed that they gave back the oxen. Then St Neot let the deer go back into the forest, but from that day a white mark like a collar appeared round the neck of each of the deer and they were protected from any huntsmen that came that way.

In the Middle Ages they thought St Neot was so holy that some clergy from Bedfordshire came and stole his relics, took them back to Bedford (doubtless pursued by angry Cornishmen), and founded a Neot's Church at the other end of the country. St Neot must have been a good man!

The London Inn stood right beside the Church of St Neot. 'It was here that the coaches called on the way to the big city', announced Anthony. The inn was a friendly place. Behind the bar were the usual trestles with barrels resting on them. But above the bar, in a place of honour, Jamie noticed a fine silver goblet. He mentioned it to Anthony, and this is what Anthony said.

A VOYAGE WITH THE PISKEYS

Once there was a boy who worked on a farm near Porthallow. One evening he was sent by the farmer's wife on an errand to fetch some household necessities from a shop in Polperro. But by the time he was on the way home with his parcel of shopping it was dark. Then in the darkness he heard a little voice saying, 'I'm for Porthallow Green.'

'You are going my way,' thought the farmer's boy, 'so I may as well have your company', and he too cried, 'I'm for Porthallow Green.' Straight away the boy found himself on Porthallow Green, surrounded by a throng of laughing, dancing piskeys. Soon he found himself joining in with their dance.

Then after a while the piskeys cried, 'I'm for Seaton Beach.' That's between Looe and Plymouth, quite a few miles. Instead of trying to escape from them, the farmer's boy also shouted out, 'I'm for Seaton Beach', and in a moment he was whisked off to Seaton and there the piskeys danced around him again, and there he found himself again joining in with their dance.

Then after another while the piskeys' cry changed once more. This time it was, 'I'm for the King of France's cellar.' But the farmer's boy did not mind even as long a journey as that. He dropped his parcel on the beach, not far from the water's edge. Then he too cried out, 'I'm for the King of France's cellar.' Immediately he found himself in a spacious cellar, tasting the finest French wines. The piskeys then led him through rooms all so splendid that they quite dazzled him. In one of the halls they found the tables were spread for a feast. Now, though the boy was in the main an honest lad, he could not resist the temptation to bring home some souvenir of his travels, and he pocketed one of the silver goblets from the banqueting table.

Then 'I'm for Seaton Beach', cried the piskeys once more. The farm lad repeated the words and he too flew to Seaton Beach. He remembered he had left his parcel of shopping on the beach, and he was sure it would have been carried away on the tide. But when he arrived the water was still a few feet away. So, just in time, he ran and picked up the parcel. Then the next destination was Porthallow. There the piskeys left him, and he went in to deliver his parcel to the farmer's wife.

'How quick you've been,' she said.

'You'd say that twice if you knew where I've been,' said the boy, 'I've been with the piskeys to Seaton, and I've been to the King of France's palace, all in five minutes.'

The farmer said, 'You must be 'mazed. Have you been at the cider?'

'I thought you'd say that,' replied the lad, 'so I brought this to show you.'

Then from his pocket he producing the silver goblet, and they all knew that his story must have been true. That goblet was an heirloom of the lad's family for generations.

33

Tardhek Warn Ugens

TRESLEA DOWNS

Next Anthony and Jamie continued on the old road to the west. Soon they passed Crows' Pound where, every Sunday, St Neot magically impounded the pilfering crows that stole grain while his parishioners were in church. The travellers crossed the swift-flowing River Bedalder at Pantersbridge and, climbing out of the wooded valley, they reached Treslea Downs and there they rested. From this high vantage point Jamie looked south over a deep river valley.

'That will be the Fowey,' said Anthony, 'that's Tristan and Iseult country that is: from the Fowey to the Fal. There are dozens of stories about Tristan and Iseult; every storyteller in medieval Britain probably had a go! Most say it's about the power of love, but I think it's about the power of music. Tristan was a fine harper, and you know what they say – "music is the food of love".'

TRISTAN AND ISEULT

Once there was a young nobleman called Tristan; he was the son of the sister of the King of Cornwall and he lived in Lyonesse. But sadly his mother died in childbirth and his father was killed in battle. So Tristan was raised by his mother's faithful servant and as a young man

*he joined the court of his uncle, King Mark
at Castle Dore. As he grew he learned all
the courtly skills, first to be a page, then a
squire and then a knight. But one morning,
when he was a young man, Tristan was
woken by cries of alarm and weeping.*

*A cry echoed across the land. 'The black
sails are coming. There is a shadow on the sea.'
Tristan saw the ships. In the bow of the fleetest
stood Morold, champion of Ireland; a grim
figurehead.*

*'Tribute I claim. Tribute I demand', he cried.
Tristan saw King Mark's servants rounding up young
men and women.*

'What is this?' asked Tristan.

*The answer came, 'Thirty young men and thirty maidens, slaves and
whores for the King of Ireland. The tribute is always paid, for no one
dare face Morold.'*

'Wait,' said Tristan, 'I will pay the tribute.'

*Morold's ship was moored at an island in the River Fowey. Tristan
called the wind and sailed there.*

'Morold,' he cried, 'I bring tribute from the people of Kernow.'

'What tribute?' said Morold, 'You are but one.'

*'In Kernow we have a saying, "onan hag oll", one and all. I am one.
I am all. I am the tribute of Kernow.'*

*With that Tristan drew his battle sword. The fight was long and hard.
Not one, not two, but three hours they fought before either man could
gain the upper hand. Then Morold's sword just touched Tristan's arm.*

'A scratch', said Tristan.

*'But enough for the poison to work', Morold laughed. 'No one knows
the cure but my sister, the Queen, and she will never help you.' He was
still laughing when Tristan's sword buried itself in his skull.*

*Then Tristan, growing ever weaker, sailed to Ireland, to the castle
of the Queen, the only one who could cure the poison. Tristan was
disguised as a minstrel. He said he had been bitten by a snake and he
begged for healing.*

The Queen was impressed; the minstrel was noble for one close to death. She gave her beautiful daughter, Iseult, the task of nursing him, and in that time their eyes met more than once. Too soon, it seemed, with his wounds healed, Tristan sailed back to Cornwall.

But the fair face of Iseult stayed in Tristan's mind. He wrote a poem telling of her beauty, but he left the parchment on his desk. There Mark found it and he was thrilled by what he read. 'Tristan', he said, 'with royal honour comes royal duty. Return to Ireland. Seek the hand of Iseult, so she may be my Queen.'

So for a second time Tristan arrived in Ireland, this time to ask for the hand of Iseult on behalf of his King. Iseult was delighted at the prospect of being a Queen in her own right and her mother was pleased that such a good match had been made. But that very night the body of Morold was at last returned and immediately both the Queen and Princess Iseult vowed vengeance upon his killer. It was sharp-eyed Iseult that noticed a small piece of metal lodged in the skull of Morold. Clearly it had come from the blade that gave him his death blow. She kept it, hoping that one day it might lead to his killer.

Soon came the day for Iseult to sail to Cornwall for her marriage. Tristan called the wind and called the waves, and a fair wind sped the ship on its way. Soon the coast of Ireland was beyond the horizon. But on the voyage the Princess Iseult noticed Tristan's sword in its scabbard, and like all women, she could not resist having a look at it! Then when she looked at the blade she noticed there was a piece missing; and it matched exactly the fragment from her uncle's skull. Clearly Tristan was no ordinary minstrel. Tristan must have been her uncle's killer, and her sworn duty was vengeance; but all around were Tristan's sailors. She decided her only honourable course was to kill Tristan and take her own life before she too was killed.

But how could she kill Tristan? Iseult had no sword, no dagger. But she did have crystals of poison hidden among her healing potions. Iseult told her maid-servant, Branwen, to distract Tristan. Then Iseult slipped the poison crystals into a flask of wine. She said, 'Let us drink a toast: to fate.'

'Why do you look so sad?' asked Tristan.

'I'm not sad,' she said, 'it's nothing but a shadow on the sea.'

Then together they drank the poisoned wine, one expecting life, the other expecting death. Soon their heads were spinning. But someone else on that ship had sworn a solemn oath. It was Branwen, Iseult's maid-servant. As a condition of service Branwen had promised Iseult's mother, the Queen of Ireland, she would keep Iseult from harm. The Queen had given Branwen crystals to make a love potion for Iseult and King Mark. So, when Iseult's back was turned, Branwen swapped the crystals. Instead of poison, Tristan and Iseult drank a love potion. Immediately they fell passionately in love.

So, arriving in Cornwall, Iseult was married to King Mark, but because of the magic potion she was in love with Tristan. Then one evening courtiers overheard Tristan and Iseult planning to meet in an orchard called Nansavallen, and those courtiers told the King. So King Mark went to the orchard and hid in a tree. But that night the moon was very bright. Looking from the ground, among the dappled shadows of the branches Tristan saw the moon-shadow of the King. He ran to the stream nearby and in it he floated first bark and then, separately, honeysuckle. It was a code to tell Iseult, who was waiting downstream, that there was something to separate her from Tristan. So when they met it was as if by accident; their conversation was brief and formal. The shadowy figure hidden in the branches was content, at least until the next rumour.

Still suspicious, Mark told his courtiers to put flour on the ground around Iseult's bower. But in the moonlight Tristan saw the flour and leapt over it into the arms of his lover. Next morning there were no footprints in the flour, but there was blood. That night Mark summoned Tristan, 'Will you not play your harp for us?' Tristan played, but the leap over the flour-laced ground had opened his old wound. As each note left the strings of his harp, a drop of blood escaped his bandages and fell to the floor. 'Proof enough', said King Mark. Guards seized Tristan and he was condemned to be burned at the stake. Iseult was to be subjected to an ordeal.

By tradition the condemned man was allowed say a last prayer at a chapel on a headland. The chapel had just one door and one narrow window over a sheer drop to the sea. Tristan persuaded his guards to let him go in alone. But then Tristan bundled the priest aside, leapt from the window and went tumbling down the cliff.

Iseult's ordeal was to be held at Kea, in the wood of the charcoal burners. To get there they had to cross the Truro River at a difficult ford, known as the Mal Pas. It is known as Malpas to this very day; 'Mopus', that's how the locals say it. All the world meets there at the river crossing: traveller, trader, priest and pilgrim. Iseult looked with horror at the ford but then a pilgrim at the water's edge called out, 'Why so sad my lady?'

'How shall I cross?' she said. Then the pilgrim declared that what was good enough for our Lord should be good enough for his lady. She should follow the example of good St Christopher, so the pilgrim carried her across on his back.

When King Mark questioned her, Iseult laughed and said that no other man had been between her thighs but the poor pilgrim who carried her over the Mal Pas. Then she seized the red-hot iron. The watchers gasped; her hand was unscathed and it proved she had told the truth. King Mark looked around and ordered his soldiers to find the pilgrim. But that pilgrim had vanished into the forest he had known as a boy, there to recover from his long fall into the sea and the stress of watching the ordeal, and there to wrestle with his conscience once again.

Many years later, at Mark's castle a banging was heard on the door. At the gate was a minstrel. He was soaked to the skin; he shivered with cold and hunger. In accordance with the ancient laws of hospitality he was shown a place by the fire and given food and drink. Then the minstrel was asked if he would entertain the court, as thanks for the hospitality he had received. He tuned his harp and started to play, and the court was stunned with the beauty of his playing. 'Sing to me', said Queen Iseult. But when the minstrel sang, King Mark recognised the verses. They were those verses he had read long ago from a parchment on a desk in his own palace, verses praising the young Iseult, then Princess of Ireland. Mark realised who the minstrel was. The music stopped as Mark's knife pressed against Tristan's neck. Then guards seized Tristan and placed him on horseback. They did not stop until they reached the River Tamar. There a proclamation was read declaring Tristan to be exiled forever and a day.

So Tristan left the granite land of Cornwall. He sailed far and became renowned as one of the great seafarers of Britain. From that day Iseult put a candle in her window every night just in case a weary sailor should need a light to guide him to landfall. To this very day, on the coast of Cornwall, a sailor's wife will always leave a candle in the window until her husband returns.

But Iseult's sailor did not return. Travel he might, but he could find no solace. Finally wind and wave carried Tristan to Brittany. To try and forget the past he took a wife, but the marriage was never consummated. When his wife challenged him Tristan found an excuse, for a great dragon was laying waste the land.

Tristan went out to face the dragon, and when it saw Tristan it rushed headlong into battle. Its fiery breath charred his shield, so all that was left was rim and boss. Tristan's great battle sword thrust and parried with consummate skill. But there was a nick in the blade, where many years before it had cleaved the skull of Morold. The blade was fatally weakened and as the dragon attacked a second time, the sword buckled as it was thrust against the dragon's scaly side, leaving no more than a scratch. A third time the dragon attacked. Now Tristan had no shield. Now Tristan had no sword. The dragon clawed and lunged. Its poisonous breath was heavy with sulphur. Tristan's head was spinning with the poison. Somehow he steadied himself, and he threw himself into the dragon's embrace. As the great talons clawed at his body, Tristan took his court sword, little more than a knife, and thrust it into the dragon's heart. The creature screamed in pain, then the flames grew weak and it fell to the ground.

Tristan, himself badly wounded, fell on the creature in agony. It was clear he would die unless nursed by someone with great skill. There was only one person in all the world who had such healing skills. Tristan sent for Iseult, who alone could save him. Tristan told his messenger that when he returned he should hoist white sails if Iseult was on board, black sails if she were not.

But his new wife overheard this instruction. When the ship appeared, the white sails reflected in the blue sea, the white sails gleamed against the blue of the sky. Tristan was too weak to move, but he could hear the ravens circling overhead and he knew the ship was in sight.

'The sails,' he whispered, 'what colour are the sails?

His jealous wife looked at the white sails. She turned to Tristan, 'There is a shadow on the sea, the sails are black.'

Then Tristan turned his face to the wall. They say he died of a broken heart, not of his wounds. Iseult landed and ran from the shore. But had a thousand Iseults run from the shore they were all too late. She held her lover's lifeless hand and she kissed his clay-cold lips as her own pulse faded and she died of grief that engulfed her, just as passion overwhelmed her in years past.

Tristan and Iseult made one last voyage together. They were brought back to Cornwall and were buried by the Chapel of St Sampson. From their graves grew a rose and a briar, which entwined so they could not be parted by any means, and as often as they were cut down they grew together again. Above Fowey a memorial stone to Tristan stands to this very day.

34

Peswardhek Warn Ugens

BODMIN

Leaving Treslea Downs and continuing on the old road to the west, they soon passed the ruins of Cardinham Castle. '"Ker Dinham": it means Dinham's castle', announced Anthony. Then he continued approvingly, 'Must have been good, they had their own minstrels.'

It was evening when they arrived in Bodmin and there they made their way towards the Assembly Rooms. A small building, it was packed; the crowd overflowed onto the street. On the road outside they met a kindly man; his collar told that he was a priest.

The priest spoke, 'Anthony James, the crowder, is that you?'

'That is my name and my profession', said Anthony, 'but I'm afraid I don't recognize your voice.'

'John Skinner, Reverend John Skinner', said the priest. 'I'm on a West Country tour. All the way from Somerset to Cornwall; my destination is Falmouth. As I travel I'm writing a journal. My friend William Sandys told me you were a fiddler and a storyteller. I was hoping you might play at the assembly tonight.'

With difficulty they made their way into the Assembly Rooms. But it seemed that there was a visiting regiment billeted in the town. Anthony had been forgotten and the regimental band had been asked to play for the dance. But the band was huge and took up half the room. The volume of the music would have been fine on a battlefield, but in Bodmin Assembly Rooms it was deafening.

As a social event it may have succeeded, for the ladies of the town seemed enchanted by the gallant young soldiers, even if conversation was impossible. But as a dance it was a disaster. John Skinner could be heard remonstrating with the master of ceremonies, 'You'd be better off with the blind fiddler and that "young scraper", the ones that usually play.'

Eventually a short, fat man approached them. He introduced himself, 'Hicks is the name, schoolmaster. I'm afraid there's no work for you here tonight.' His eyes twinkled, 'Come with me to the Hole in the Wall, we can have some supper. Then perhaps we could swap a few a stories?'

Anthony whispered to Jamie, 'They call him the Yorick of the West!'

In the inn they dined well, for Hicks was a generous and genial host. 'Kindness is never misplaced', he said. Then Hicks started to speak. His tales were works of art, told with great skill. Every point was sharpened, every detail considered. Also, like Anthony, he sang songs and accompanied himself on the fiddle. Soon many people gathered round, for Hicks had great skill at telling a long story and keeping his hearers thrilled throughout, breathless lest they should lose a word. Anthony too was attentive, for to be a good storyteller you must also be a good listener.

THE PISKEY THRESHER

The north coast of Cornwall is wild and rugged. But the south coast has lower cliffs, and above them farmland rolls down towards the sea. On the south coast there is one place I could show you where it always seems that the crops are good, and in the late summer the waves on the ocean are echoed by waves wind-blown in golden fields.

But it was it not always so. Once the land was farmed by an old widow-woman and her young son, Jack. The old woman was wise to the ways of the land; she understood the soil and the seasons. One of her many instructions was always to leave a little something for the piskeys. She used to say:

Kind hearts are gardens,
Kind thoughts are roots,
Kind words are blossoms,
Kind deeds are fruits.

But often times were difficult and they had hardly enough for themselves. But still her son always followed his mother's instructions and always left a saucer of milk or some scraps of bread in the barn, just in case the little people were in need.

Then one magic year young Jack sowed his corn-seed. As he sowed he sang:

One for the rook, one for the crow,
One to rot and one to grow.

But the rook said to the crow:

Fly away Peter, fly away Paul,
Piskey says take none at all.

And the sun said to the warm earth:

> *Sun and rain and growing seed,*
> *August harvest gold indeed.*

When the first green shoots appeared it was clear that they would have a bumper harvest. Jack said to himself, 'How shall I ever get such a harvest safe in the barn before the rains come?' When the harvest field shone gold he went out at dawn with his scythe and with slow steady strokes worked until dusk. But the field was large and in the last light of the day he saw he had only cut about a quarter of it. As he gathered in the stooks that were ready, he sighed as he saw the clouds on the horizon.

But when Jack awoke next morning and looked from the window he saw that the whole field had been cut. He ran to the barn and saw it was full. As if by magic the harvest was ready for threshing, to loosen the wheat from the chaff. So Jack took his threshel to beat the grain on the threshing floor. But the barn was large, and in the last light of day he saw he had only threshed about a quarter of the grain. He sighed as he realised he could never get his harvest threshed and winnowed and sacked in time for market.

But when Jack woke the next morning and went to the barn he saw that all the threshing had been done. As if by magic all the grain was ready for winnowing. So Jack opened the doors either end of the barn so that the wind blew through. Then he took his winnowing fork and began tossing the grain so the light chaff was carried away on the wind, and the heavy grain collected at his feet. When there was enough he shovelled the grain into a sack. All day he winnowed and sacked. But the harvest was large, and in the last light of day he saw he had only winnowed about a quarter of it. He sighed as he realised he could never get his grain winnowed and sacked in time for market, which was the very next day.

But in the middle of the night Jack suddenly woke up. He put on a dressing gown and crept down the stairs. Without making a sound, Jack tip-toed out to the barn. The doors had been opened, but he carefully looked in through a crack in the planking. Inside he saw a little man, clad in a tattered green jacket. This little fellow was wielding a winnowing fork unlike one Jack had ever seen. The fork moved so swiftly it was almost invisible. Sack after sack of grain was filled and put on the cart.

So when he woke the next morning and returned to the barn he saw that all the winnowing and sacking was done. All the sacks of grain were on the cart ready to be taken to the market. So in the first light of the day, off he went to market, and there he got an excellent price for his grain. Then the very next thing he did was go to the tailor's shop. 'I want the finest jacket you can make,' said Jack, 'but it must be green, and must fit a little man only about two feet high.' The tailor looked very surprised, but he made the jacket just as he was asked.

That night before Jack went to bed he went out to the barn. There he left a little jug of milk, some bread and cheese, and beside it he left the green jacket. Then Jack went to bed, but in the middle of the night he woke up. Once again he put on his dressing gown and he went tip-toeing out to the barn. There, as he peered inside, he saw the little chap drink up the milk, eat the bread and cheese and, with a huge smile on his face, try on the jacket. Jack smiled too as he saw that the jacket fitted perfectly. Then the little man started to sing:

Piskey fine, and piskey gay,
Piskey now will fly away.

Then the little man ran out into the darkness, and he was never seen again. But still Jack always left what he could for the little people. And to this very day on the south coast there is a place I could show you, where it always seems that the crops are good, and in the late summer the waves on the ocean are echoed by waves wind-blown in golden fields.

35

Pempthek Warn Ugens

CARMINNOW CROSS

The moors above Bodmin were white with frost. The days were now noticeably shorter and summer was in headlong retreat. Anthony said it was the wings of the Winter Raven, shadowing the earth ever longer as he reached the peak of his powers. In a derelict chapel east of the town, Anthony and Jamie shivered by a small fire.

'The snow will soon be falling on the high ground', said Anthony. 'You're lucky down on the Lizard, it hardly ever snows. Mind you, it has enough wind and rain instead! I never saw snow until I was ten years old.

THE OLD GOOSE-WOMAN

My grandma used to tell me that above the clouds lived the Old Goose-Woman of the Sky. In winter she would pluck her goose; the snow was the falling feathers. I always wanted to climb a high mountain to see if I could see the old woman. I used to ask my grandma where she lived.

'She has a cottage in the sky', said my grandma.

'Where does she keep the goose?' I would ask.

'In the sky meadows, up above the clouds', grandma would reply.

'Really?' I said.

One day I asked my gran what the old woman would do when she finished plucking her goose. Grandma replied abruptly, 'Why, stuff her with onions and sage of course!'

'What then?'

'Roast her for Christmas dinner!'

'Poor old goose', I said. 'Are you sure you've got it right? I don't think the old woman would be so cruel as to kill and pluck the goose that's been her companion all year.'

'What do you think?' asked my grandma.

'I think that winter is the moulting time of the great Sky Goose. Then the old Goose-Woman has to sweep out the feathers from her cottage, and they come floating down to earth.'

'Anthony James,' said Grandma, 'I do believe you're a storyteller!'

The Parting of the Ways

The next morning dawned cloudy. Anthony James walked briskly up the long hill beyond the town, heading towards a watery sun. Jamie struggled to keep up with Anthony. 'Slow down, Dad!' he called.

'What did you say?' asked Anthony.

'Slow down!' laughed Jamie.

'No, after that.'

'Dad?' said Jamie. 'Oh, I'm sorry. The words just came out.'

'Did you guess?' asked Anthony.

'It just seemed right', said his son.

At the top of the rise the horizons opened out and framed the sky. To the north and north-east were the hills of Bodmin Moor. To the west was the downland above St Breock, to the south the rolling moors above St Austell, with the great mound of Hensbarrow standing guard. To the east was the wooded valley of the River Fowey, winding from Bodmin Moor down to the Channel. Every horizon guarded a harvest of memories, stories and songs.

Ahead lay the crest of the hill. Beyond it the road dropped down into the deep river valley. Anthony James paused at a wayside cross

that stood tall on the horizon. The cross was carved from ancient granite; it looked as if it had stood there, battling the elements, forever. The cross-head was wheel-shaped in the old Celtic fashion. The sun gathered strength. To Jamie, his father's silhouette merged with that of stone pillar. When he spoke it could have been the granite speaking.

'Jamie, I love you,' he said, 'but now I am going to a place you cannot follow. I must make my way across the great river. Winter is coming and I can no longer walk the lanes and sleep under the stars. Soon the giants will reclaim the moors, piskeys will own the fields and mermaids will rule the ocean. No more will they heed my words. Soon the old Goose-Woman will be sending handfuls of cold feathers from the skies. I must go to the place where old soldiers go. You still have much to learn, but you know my tunes and my tales. I can teach you no more. For now you must go and look after your mother. Come the spring you can take the road again. You can tell my tales, play my tunes. I'll not be far away.'

Anthony placed his hands on his son's shoulders. He kissed his son and swiftly turned. He strode down the road, perhaps not quite at his usual pace. Although the leaves were now yellow and golden, and many lay on the ground, the trees by the River Fowey still cast deep shadows beyond which nothing could be seen. The sound of the river seemed to grow louder, masking the sounds of all beyond it. At the bend before the bridge, Anthony James turned and waved.

'Tell 'em for me', he shouted. Then he was gone.

36

CURY

BIRDSONG

It took Jamie three days to walk from Bodmin to Cury, even though he hurried, much as the autumn leaves scurried at his feet. He walked quickly, not only to get home as soon as possible, but also to keep warm, as now the days were cold as well as the nights. Many trees were bare under the relentless onslaught of the western gale, and the wind made Jamie's eyes water. At least that's what he told those who asked. But his grief at parting from Anthony faded when he saw the familiar fields and hedges, and then the hamlet of Cury itself.

The cottage was strangely silent. Although it was early evening there was no light. Gingerly, Jamie pushed open the door. He called out softly, 'Mum? Mother?'

There was no answer, but Jamie sensed a movement from the kitchen. There in the half-darkness Martha was slumped forward in an upright chair, weeping into her pinafore. The baby slept in the cot by the window.

'Oh Jamie, thank goodness you've come. Vingoe, he's dead.' Again she buried her head in her hands.

Jamie said nothing, stunned at the news of his step-father. He took his mother in his arms and held her tight. Martha spoke again, 'There was a fight, up at Cury Great Tree. You know, on the knoll where the Helston and Mawgan roads cross. There was a wreck down on the Lizard and a party of Wendron men went down to see what they could take. On the way back, at the Great Tree, they met another gang from Breage. Of course, they fought over the spoils didn't they? Some people never learn. They were all armed with staves; the constable said that the road ran red with the blood. Somehow Vingoe was in the middle of it. He was knocked to the ground and then hit on the head with a patten iron. It's not safe to go into Helston after dark now, they still fight over it.'

'Oh Mother,' said Jamie, 'I am so very sorry', and together they wept.

It was a hard, sad winter. Jamie's meagre earnings were soon exhausted. He took jobs wherever he could. Martha took in washing. William Sandys paid Jamie well for fiddling and singing carols, and somehow they survived. Christmas was a muted affair, though the parishioners were kind enough. 'Anything but Helston workhouse', said Martha, grimly.

She was pleased to see the green shoots and hear the birdsong of spring. It was a time to plant, a time to grow, a time to begin again.

One spring morning full of promise and birdsong, Jamie walked up the lane from Cury towards White Cross. The day was sky-bright and clear, but Jamie's mind was numb to the new energy that flooded into the awakening year. As his feet crunched on the gravel the boy became aware of the distant, pervasive sound of the sea. Something prompted Jamie's eyes to focus on the dry-stone wall beside him. He saw that, as the wall approached the hamlet, the irregular field-stones had given way to a neater, vertical pattern. He ran his finger across the stones.

'That'll be the town hedge', said a voice behind him. Jamie started with surprise, then screamed at the top of his voice, 'Anthony! I thought… I thought I never… I… I love you.'

'And I love you, Jamie', said Anthony James. 'I know what I said. But I thought, "one more time, just one more time". And then I had this powerful feeling that you needed me. So I started walking and here I am.' He continued, 'Let me put my hand on your shoulder, just like before. Please Jamie, take me home'.

The sun was at their backs as they walked down from the direction of White Cross. The old man's clothes were weather-beaten as ever; you could hardly tell that once they had been military uniform. Over his shoulder was the same old canvas sack. At his left side the green cloth bag hung from his belt.

Half a mile later, they stopped at the small cottage. The low thatched roof was still in need of attention and a wisp of smoke still curled from the chimney. Then Anthony opened the bag and from it took his violin. He put it to his chin and drew the bow across the strings. The music was swift and light, but soulful all the same. The notes echoed through the open door.

From inside there was a cry that was a laugh and a shout all together, and Martha ran to the door, a toddler on her hip.

'Anthony James,' she cried, 'thank God you've come.' Their embrace was long; full of smiles and tears. 'Would you have a cup of nettle tea?' said Martha, remembering times past.

'Martha,' said Anthony, 'there are two things a man should never refuse from a good woman, and the first of them is a cup of tea.'

'You old rogue,' she said, 'what's the second?'

'Another cup of tea, of course,' he replied, 'what did you expect?'

That night was clear and still, and the stars were very bright. It seemed that the evening star hung only just beyond the window pane. The sound of the sea was in the distance, but from a small tree nearby called a rare and precious bird, and its song filled the heavens. Safe in his bed, Jamie remembered the story of Odysseus. In that famous tale, when the hero returned to his wife Penelope after ten years of wandering, Athena held back the dawn in order to prolong the loving couple's night together. Now Jamie wished it could be so once again.

Sources

William Bottrell (1816-1881) of St Levan, later lived near St Ives. His tales, gathered from his family and from local miners, first appeared in the *Cornish Telegraph* from 1867. He previously communicated over fifty 'drolls' to Hunt, and they appeared in *Hunt's Popular Romances of the West of England* of 1865. The then editor of the *Cornish Telegraph* suggested to Bottrell that he should write and publish the stories himself:

Bottrell, W., *Traditions and hearthside stories of West Cornwall* (Penzance, W. Cornish for the author, 1870)

Bottrell, W., *Traditions and hearthside stories of West Cornwall, Second Series* (Penzance, Beare & Son for the author, 1873)

Bottrell, W., *Traditions and hearthside stories of West Cornwall, Third Series* (Penzance, F. Rodda for the author, 1880)

Margaret Ann Courtney (1834 – date unknown) lived in Penzance in the late nineteenth century. Her work originally appeared as a series of articles in *Folklore*, the journal of the Folklore Society, 1886-1887:

Courtney, M.A., *Cornish Feasts and Folk-Lore* (Penzance, Beare, 1890)

Robert Hunt (1807-1887) was a scientist and antiquarian. Schooled in London, by 1829 he had settled in Cornwall, his mother's county of birth, due to ill health. His tales came from his mother, from an early interest in folklore, and from William Bottrell. Hunt, however, has different versions of many of Bottrell's tales and much original material:

Hunt, R., *Popular Romances of the West of England* (two volumes) (J. C. Hotten, London, 1865)

Enys Tregarthen was the pseudonym of **Nellie Sloggett** (1851-1923) of Padstow who collected and published many stories about the piskey folk:

Tregarthen, E., *The Piskey-Purse. Legends and tales of North Cornwall* (London, Wells Gardner & Co.,1905)

Tregarthen, E., *North Cornwall Fairies and Legends* (London, Wells Gardner & Co.,1906)

Tregarthen, E., *The House of the Sleeping Winds, and other stories, some based on Cornish folklore...* (London, Rebman, 1911)

William Frederick Collier (1824-1902) was the chronicler of William Hicks of Bodmin:

Collier, W.F., *Tales and Sayings of William Hicks of Bodmin* (Truro, Joseph Pollard, 1903)

Both **Sabine Baring Gould** (1834-1924) and **Robert Stephen Hawker** (1803-1875) refer to Cornish folk tales and legends:

Baring Gould, S. *A Book of the West. II: Cornwall* (London, Methuen, 1899)

Hawker, R.S., *Cornish Ballads and Other Poems* (London, Bodley Head, 1869)

Baring Gould's biography of **Hawker** provides a useful overview:

Baring Gould, S., *The Vicar of Morwenstow: A Life of Robert Stephen Hawker, M.A.* (London, Henry S. King, 1876)

Many Cornish tales were kept alive in literature in the retellings including:

Couch, M., *Cornwall's Wonderland* (London, J. M. Dent, 1914)

'Lyonesse' (possibly Barham, G. B.), *Legend Land, being a collection of some of the OLD TALES told in those Western Parts of Britain served by The Great Western Railway* (four volumes) (London, The Great Western Railway, 1922 and 1923)

Enys, Sarah L., *Cornish Drolls, Compiled from Bottrell* (Plymouth, W. Brendon & Son, 1931)

Rawe, Donald, *Traditional Cornish Stories and Rhymes* (Padstow, Lodenek Press, 1971)